# In the Shadows of the Whispering Pines

**David Chaltas**

**In the Shadows of the Whispering Pines**

Title ID: 3891874
ISBN-13:978-1477553152
Library of Congress: Pending

Front cover image by permission of:
**Doug and Suzan Stiles, owners of
Pine Ridge Lodge Bed & Breakfast
2730 Pine Haven Road
Lewiston, Michigan 49756**
www.pineridgelodgemi.com

Back cover by permission of The Stiles

David Chaltas
Deer Branch Road
Box 41
Jeremiah, Kentucky 41826
honestlee33@yahoo.com

Proudly
Printed in the United States of America

# DEDICATION

(Pine Ridge Lodge Logo)

This book is dedicated to all those who possess shadowy childhood memories and long to find them once again. To God for His abundant goodness to this unworthy man, I praise Him. To my better half, I say thank you for supporting me and believing in me when I did not believe in myself. To my children and grandchildren, I offer this legacy in hopes that you do not make the mistakes of the father.

I present my sincerest gratitude to Doug and Suzan Anthony-Stiles, owners and innkeepers of Pine Ridge Lodge, who graciously allowed me to stay in my childhood cabin during my period of rediscovery and saw the vision of the lodge. They also assisted me in the research of the lodge's history. To my youthful friends of yesteryear, may God have richly blessed your life as He has mine. To the Smiths for their kindness to a child of promise, I offer my undying gratitude, love and devotion. To Mrs. Marie Smith, I offer my sincerest appreciation for her years of guidance.

Finally, to my dear mother, Dana Blair, I express total appreciation for our times in the pines.

(Mother at Little Bear Lake in Sept. 1956)
(Camping and Fishing)

# FOREWORD

I have heard the sound of whispering pines all my life. Though I didn't understand their words, I knew they were calling me home. It started at the age of five when I first saw the majesty of the pine forest and heard the mighty AuSable River singing to me to come and drink from her cold waters. For approximately six years I listened to the murmurs of the whispering pines, not understanding the language or the pining of the spirit. Was it the sounds of the woods that lured me back or that of an unfulfilled childhood? Was it the inexplicable joy I experienced during those days in Camelot? Would my destiny have been different had I lingered amongst the pines or have I indeed found my purpose? Were the blessings of knowing a loving family in those younger years preparing me and forging within me strength to withstand the torrents of a troubled dysfunctional family life in my latter years? I have a tendency to think so and praise God for both. All I know is that once again I have heard the pines call my name and I must beckon to their call.

For me, this manuscript is a journey of reflection. It is a saga of a time gone by that I carry in my heart. In reality, it represents a time that ALL of us longingly embrace; the time of our youth. How wondrous to have precious memories that no one can take away. They belong to each of us and yet to all of us. They are, in essence, what has molded us, shaped us, into the unique creation we have become. Without knowing our past; the things we were, we cannot truly know ourselves.

So, dear reader, this is my road to rediscovery, redefinition, and recovery of memories long ago lost or forgotten. I am sure the passageway will be filled with sweet reminiscences, melancholy memories, and lessons I dread to face. Already my mind is saturated with faded memories that wish to be expressed but fear of finding the truth about my greatest enemy, which has held my spirit for so long. That enemy is my own self esteem and doubts of worthiness. I often think of the 'what ifs' in life, but have come to realize that God's plan for my life as well as yours will be revealed, if you listen to the sounds of the whispering pines.

I ask you to come along with me as I relive those days of yesterday by revisiting a bygone era, after being absent for over fifty years. As in my youth, I was filled with the flames of life fashioned while under the shadows of the whispering pines. I remain your obedient servant, David Chaltas

Proverbs 22:6

"Train up a child in the way he should go and when he is old, he will not depart from it."

# ABOUT THE AUTHOR

David Philip Chaltas is a prolific writer who resides in eastern Kentucky. He was selected Teacher of the Year by the Council of Children with Behavioral Disorders. He is the first recipient of such a prestigious honor in the state of Kentucky. His innovative Education Program won the coveted 2000-2001 Program of the Year by the International Association of Directors of Pupil Personnel. He was presented with the award in Orlando, Florida. He has been a State Consultant on Emotional Behavioral Disorders and established a pilot program to meet the needs of those students. He is a Kentucky Colonel as well as an ordained minister who has served in the capacity of the Kentucky Division Chaplain for the Sons of Confederate Veterans. He served as the Army of Tennessee Chaplain, which covers eleven states. He is a proud Veteran of Foreign Wars, having served during the Vietnam struggle. He is an accomplished retired musician who decided to write the words for future generations to read.

His writings have been published in several magazines and newspapers including The Civil War Courier (a national newspaper), The Civil War Gazette (national magazine), The Kentucky Explorer, Lost Cause, East Kentucky Magazine, "Tree Huggin" John's Ezine, Appalachian Quarterly (he was selected as the Civil War Correspondent), and Letcher County Historical

Society publications. He has served as the Commander of the Colonel Ben Caudill #1629 Sons of Confederate Veterans, Commander of the Cumberland Brigade, and a member of the Southern Guard Battalion, Tennessee Valley Battalion, Armies of Tennessee, Kentucky Cavalry Brigade, Hardee's Corps, North/South Alliance and Cleburne Division reenacting group. He has been featured nationally in the persona of General Robert E. Lee at numerous reenactments. He has written three quality plays that have been well received. He was chosen to represent General Lee at the 2005 National Reunion. He was selected to be the keynote speaker at the Lee/Jackson Day event, held in Lexington, Virginia, honoring the 200th birthday of Robert E. Lee. He has spoken at Annapolis, MD; during the memorial service for the marines buried at St. Ann's Cemetery and offered a presentation at the church. He was honored by being selected to present at Francis Scott Keys cemetery in Maryland, and was the keynote speaker in Columbia, South Carolina, at the annual state capitol rally.

His persona of Robert Edward Lee brings to life living history, as he offers inspiring presentations for churches, schools, civic organizations, memorial services, dedications, and reenactments. He follows the old path and the drums of yesteryear.

# AUTHOR'S NOTES

Once in a lifetime you have a mission or goal that might not be the world's greatest contribution to the world but for the person involved with the mission, it is a complete catharsis. In perusing the Shadows of the Whispering Pines, I rediscovered such a self awareness of my identity, an awakening and renewal, along with a total liberation of my spirit. The release of memories was likened unto a beaver's dam bursting. It served to wash away some of the pain of not remembering and reflections of what might have been. The outpouring offered a sweet release and renewed hope for the future. Suddenly it donned upon my being the realization of my unique childhood. How it forged the man became crystal clear. I found the memoirs of my early days sustained me and helped me recommit to embrace the new shadows that remain in my future. On the wings of a prayer, I began my voyage in July of 2010. Though very personal, I felt it of the essence to share, in hopes that someday it will help you, dear reader, recall the sounds heard during your time of youth when you played in the shadows of the whispering pines.

## BOOKS BY THE AUTHOR:

Lessons for Life
This Old Book
When Ravens Dance
The Search for Butternut
Appalachian Rebels
Brothers Once More
The Legend and Legacy of Lee
The Fading of the Gray
Poetry of the Civil War
Good Kids-Bad Behavior
Mourning in the Mountains
The Diaper Tree
When You Follow Your Heart
ABC'S of Appalachian Expressions
Tears in the River
Just Over the Dawn
An Open Book for Closed Minds
The Book of Books
General Dispatches
The General's Journal
The General's Dispatch
Confederate Kin I & II
Alpha and Omega of Sayings
Native American Sayings, Customs and Prayers
Shadows of Gettysburg
Four Women: One War

# TABLE OF CONTENTS

## CHAPTERS

(Driveway leading to Pine Ridge Lodge)

# SHADOWED MEMORIES

It has been said you can never go home. It has been stated that the skeletons of the past need to remain in the mind's closet. Maybe there is some truth in the sayings but something bigger than life compelled me to begin a new search for my stolen youth regardless of the cost. Was the greatest lesson for life, which would hopefully offer closure to so many unanswered questions, waiting for me after fifty-two years of ponderings? Would the shadows of the whispering pines disclose the secrets of yesterday? What would those majestic pines tell me about my youth? Would they remain silent or offer the whispers that could not be understood by a mere mortal? Could or would they share shadowed memories?

Sometimes the greatest lessons for life are those you are reluctant to learn. My lesson was a journey back to my childhood. Shadowed memories fade in and out of the sun, as I made the trip to Red Oak, Michigan, where I spent six years of my youth. My mind was a sponge absorbing lost moments, as I began to recall the wonders, worries, and the heartbreaks of my youth. Each scene was a reflection of yesterday, though some of the secrets were lost to the dimming of the mind. Each location called anew the old experiences which had created me. I had inquiries that needed to be answered and preserved for not only my own satisfaction but also to offer insight to my children's children. I decided to keep a journal of my travels and found it to be the most challenging of my life. For written between the lines of those pieces of paper I found that I had to face my greatest fears and my worst enemy; myself.

The quest began when I was leisurely surfing the Internet, as I had done a thousand times. My search led me to typing in the name Pine Haven Lodge on the computer. The lodge was my childhood home and it was a name which I had searched on many occasions before but those attempts proved fruitless in my explorations. This time though, I noted a name close to my previous investigations and I decided to open the website. To my surprise, shock, and delight, I immediately recognized Pine Haven Lodge, which was now called Pine Ridge Lodge. The image of the large log structure was as if it stepped out of my mind's eye and posted itself on the page. I shook with anticipation and disbelief. Had it been there all this time? It brought back a stream of memories. As I wandered down the page, a small cabin came into view and I instantly knew I had once again discovered the home of my youth. It looked exactly as I remembered it in my youth and the old trees offering the cabin shade seemed to smile and say, "Welcome home son".

# THE VISIONARIES

Pine Haven Lodge was built by a man who I would come to know as "Uncle Pug". His real name was Morris Avery Smith. He was a professional boxer and had played minor league ball. He came to Northern Michigan with a vision, a dream, and of course, his family. With their bare hands, they made the dream a reality.

Uncle Pug was born on September 4, 1891. He had a twin by the name of Norris Charles Smith. They were born in Evart, Michigan. His younger brother was named after his father, Alfred. They were the sons of Alfred R. Smith and Sarah Belle Davidson Smith (circa 1865). Most records have Sarah listed as Belle. A memorial stone is located in Forest Hills, Evart, Michigan. She is buried on a plot owned by Duncan Town. Davidson was her brother-in-law. The plot is referred to as the Davidson plot and is located in section D of the cemetery. She is buried in lot 3, grave one. She died in 1932, at the age of forty-seven. Her sister, O'Della Henry, is buried in lot #4, grave 4. She was sixty eight years of age at her passing on September 19, 1937. The burial place of Alfred R. Smith remains undiscovered at this juncture.

Documents confirm that Mabel Alice Burkett was born in Homer, Michigan, in 1900. She was the daughter of Albert and Lottie Burkett. Sometime during her youth, Aunt Mabel was orphaned.

She was enrolled in an all-girl boarding school where she learned the fine art of being a lady. She carried that education with dignity and grace all through her life. Documents suggest that Mabel worked as a waitress in her younger years and later worked as a bookkeeper. On some of the United States Federal Census statements, Mabel was listed as a house wife or home maker, but she served the family by taking care of many aspects of running the lodge. She was always a lady and encouraged 'we' men to behave as gentlemen. I tried to live up to that standard but have failed on many occasions.

The 1900 United States Federal Census has Alfred listed as being thirty-three years old, Belle as age thirty-five and Morris and Norris as age nine years old. They were living in Benton Harbor (Berrin County) Michigan. The records show that Belle was born in Ohio and that Alfred R. was born in Michigan. (Source-Census Place: Benton Harbor, Berrien, Michigan; RollT623_702; page 23B, Enumeration District: 55)

The 1910 United States Federal Census record for Belle Smith shows that she was living in Port Huron Ward 11, St. Clair, Michigan, during that time period. Her sons, Morris, Norris, and Alfred were living with her during that point in time. She would have been forty-five. Her marital status is listed as divorced on the census record.

(Source-190 Census Place: Port Huron Ward 22, St. Clare, Michigan: Roll 7624_673; page: 13A; Enumeration District: 120; image 962).

Somewhere, somehow, sometime along the way, Morris and Mabel met and were later married. Their wedding date is recorded as May 10, 1917. Mabel was eight years younger than Morris. Their union produced three children.

On June 5, 1917, at the age of twenty-six, both Morris and Norris reported for the draft. Note that Morris had only been married thirty-eight days when he was called to register. On Morris's draft registration for World War I, the card shows that he was living at 1272 (?) Mason, Flint, Michigan, and was working as a store clerk. His draft registration card is 5253, no 397. His brother Norris registered on the same date and is listed as living at 221-10 Ave, Flint, Michigan. Norris Charles Smith's card is 5254, # 390. Both served during World War I.

Physical characteristics stated on the card regarding the men revealed they were tall-median to stocky built, possessing brown eyes and brown hair. This matches my memory, though I am quite sure that Aunt Mabel was taller than Uncle Pug. I believe that it was during this time frame (1910-20s) that Uncle Pug began his professional boxing career. Sometime in his younger years, Uncle Pug played ball in the minor leagues. His twin brother, Norris, was the pitcher and Uncle Pug was the catcher. I remember how hard Uncle Pug could pass the ball to me. It stung my hand until I 'toughened up' somewhat!

Noting that World War I began in 1914, and ended on November 11, 1918, it is possible that Uncle Pug and Uncle Norris served the duration of the entire war after being drafted or volunteering. Also, noting that Morris A. Smith 'Smitty' was born on August 21, 1918. It is possible that he was conceived upon Uncle Pug's reunion with his bride. Uncle Pug may have been discharged early. Morris A. 'Smitty' was the eldest, Alys (pronounced Alice) Yvonne Geiger (married surname) was born in 1920, and Donna Louise Smith was born in 1923.

The 1930 Unites States Federal Census record showed that Morris A. Smith and family resided in Flint Ward 2, Genesee County, Michigan. He was thirty-eight and Mable A. Smith was thirty. According to the document, they owned their own home. All three children (Morris A.-11 years old, Alys Yvonne-9 years old, and Donna L.-7 years old) resided with them. (Source-2920 Census Place: Flint Ward 2, Genesee, Michigan; Roll T625_765; page 5A; Enumeration District: 26; Image: 77)

On June 12, 1937, (registered at 2:00 P. M. by the county court clerk's office) Uncle Pug purchased forty+ acres of land for 'one dollar and other valuable consideration'. The land had previously been owned by Henry A. Spencer and Lois E. Spencer of Flint, Michigan. According to my friend who is an attorney, 'other valuable consideration' usually refers to love and affection, which eliminated payment of property taxes. I am not sure if this was the case but it is my premise that the Spencer's were related to the Smiths or very dear friends. (Oscoda County, Michigan Warranty Deed #464, page 23)

With age comes the fading of the gray matter. Sometimes we forget details but recall items that to others are insignificant. With that in mind, the following is what I remember about the history of the lodge.

My best recollection regarding what I overheard and or was told is that the Smith family brought a small Streamline trailer with them in order to live on the property while they worked on their dream house. It sat beside an apple tree. Uncle Pug began the laborious tasks of building the dream home by constructing a small sawmill and a make-shift kiln to dry the lumber. It was a few yards away from the trailer. Once the mill was operational, Uncle Pug and family began construction on a cabin at the foot of a small ridge where the lodge was to be constructed. He built what is known in Northern Michigan as a "long house" for his family to live while he worked on the lodge. The loggers called them long houses because of their resemblance to the Ojibwa houses.

The cabin was twelve feet wide and forty-eight feet in length, with a bedroom sixteen-foot in length. The other twenty-four feet made up the living room, dining area and kitchen. There was a small (five by five entrance way) where you took off your coat and shoes. This also provided a wind breaker area for the winter and summer months. The logs were of pine and measured eight inches in diameter. The ceilings were eighty–eight inches high. The cabin contained five windows measuring forty-four by forty-two inches. The cabin faced the east which maximized the heat from the morning sun. From 1953 to 1959, the 'long house' cabin was where the metal of this man was forged.

Uncle Pug also constructed a fine two-story garage/workshop filled with tools needed to construct the lodge of their dreams. It was quite large and was made of rounded pine poles with heavy timber beams running the length of the workshop. He built a pit where he could service his tractors that he used to pull the fallen logs up the ridge where he planned to build Pine Haven Lodge. The date inscribed on the workshop foundation is 1940.

Construction began on the lodge but soon after its completion, disaster came in the form of a fire. Most of the Smith's belongings were destroyed. But the fire did not dampen their pioneering spirit. The family decided to build on the ridge overlooking the long house, just a few yards from the garage. They began working on another lodge a few hundred yards from the original site.

One can surmise that it took him three years to get everything in readiness to begin construction on the ten-bedroom lodge. He not only built the lodge but also the furniture out of pines from the surrounding area.

I am certain his brother, Norris Charles Smith, helped in the construction of the grand lodge too. During the construction of the cabin, workshop, and lodge, there is no doubt in my mind that his lovely wife, (My dear Aunt Mabel) was right there by his side working, along with Morris A. 'Smitty or Junior', Robert Hart Geiger (Uncle Pug and Aunt Mable's son-in-law), Alys Y. Geiger, and Donna L. Smith on the lodge. There must have been other people assisting in the construction but I cannot recall any other names. An interesting side-note by Suzan Stiles is that she and Doug were told that the reason the second story is vertical instead of horizontal is one man built it, and by doing it in vertical construction, he could handle the logs all by himself. As Suzan states, *"This may or may not be true, but it's a brilliant theory."* I concur with her thinking and Uncle Pug was quite capable of such a feat.

To the best of my recollection, I am almost certain Uncle Pug informed a group of guests who were at the lodge that it had taken him over six years to complete the lodge. The men had gathered in the den and I was listening while sitting on the 'talking pole'. Until the lodge was habitable, Uncle Pug, Aunt Mabel and his family lived in the little cabin at the foot of the hill during that time frame. Later they moved into the unfinished lodge and worked on it for many laborious months.

Finally in 1948, the grand opening of the lodge occurred with much fanfare. Being one of the few establishments in the area, the lodge soon became a beacon to the targeted clientele. The lodge was built as a respite for hunters and fishermen to relax and enjoy after a day of adventure. Uncle Pug even offered guided hunting and fishing tours around his property. The grand AuSable River flows close by and there are an abundance of lakes and wildlife. The Twin Lakes are located on the outskirts of Lewiston, Michigan. Snyder, Pickerel, Muskrat, Big Wolf, Big Bear, Tea, Moon, Elmer, Oak, Spencer, and Little Bear Lakes are within minutes of the lodge. The renowned Garland Golf Course, located on County Road 489, is only minutes from the lodge. Several ponds and swift moving streams flow through the black pine, aspen, and oak forest as well. The marsh area affords fresh water to the great lakes. The AuSable runs into the mighty Lake Huron.

One trout stream important to me was between Danny's house and the restaurant known as the Rustic Inn. The Rustic Inn did not exist when I was a child but now serves as a point of reference. The stream is on the side of the road where the Inn is located. Water ran over logs from an old mill and plummeted to a swift flowing pool. It was ideal for brook and rainbow trout. I used to love to see them floating effortlessly in the cold tributary of the Au Sable River. There was a bridge in the area as well but I don't recall its exact location. We walked along the bank fishing and on many occasions we came back home with our feet soaking wet from wading the cold water.

Different hunting seasons and skiing afforded opportunity for guests to come and enjoy their quests at Pine Haven. Rabbit, deer, and bird season afforded traffic up and down the lane, as well as visitors to the lodge. The location was perfect for the lodge's design and purpose. On many occasions the hunting racks would be filled with the hunter's trophies being displayed for all to see. Sometimes I would be given a quarter to take pictures of the captured game with the hunters proudly standing beside the prey.

# THE PRIVATE RETREAT

Pine Haven lodge was sold in the early sixties to a family associated with the Pepsi Corporation. Mr. and Mrs. Glenn and Lillian Burgam had a vested interest in distribution of Pepsi and used the lodge for corporate and private retreats. Their renovations entailed adding a screened in patio, new living quarters downstairs and installing drop ceilings. They also had several of the pines cut down while owning the property. This must have been done in the early 1970s. They also built a two story garage with a caretaker's apartment overhead. They expanded the yard to include more space for their guests.

(Garage a few yards southeast of Pine Ridge Lodge)

Mr. and Mrs. Burgam attended St. Francis Church in Lewiston, Michigan, and as age approached, both were confined to a wheel chair. They had a bull dog which they kept in the house most of the time and Glenn was known to constantly smoke and chew on a cigar. In his later years he would visit the lodge and sit on the patio watching the wonders around him. It is my understanding that the caretaker never lived in the home but skillfully supervised the maintenance of the forty acres. The Burgams died in the 1980s and are buried in the St. Francis Cemetery outside of Lewiston.

Upon the deaths of the Burgams, the lodge and cabin lay empty. The grounds began to be unkempt and decay found its way into the crevices of the cabins. The property was even offered to the church where the Burgams attended but they declined to accept the gift due to the cost of preserving the structure. Due to no one living within her walls for over four years, and the lack of maintaining the grand lady, it soon began to show its age. Some of the pipes burst and the grand structure started a rapid decline due to lack of maintenance. If one listened on a clear night, the woods gave the impression that the whispering pines sighed with sorrow.

# THE VISION REDISCOVERED

Sometimes one questions their purpose in life and there comes a life altering moment in which one sees the purpose of life. That came to Suzan Anthony upon seeing the rundown lodge that she now calls home. This is her story of rejuvenation

Suzan grew up in Grayling, Michigan, and attended college at Eastern Michigan University. She received a Bachelor of Science degree in the field of psychology and criminal justice. She worked two years at the Miami County Youth Center in Troy, Ohio. She worked at a juvenile treatment and detention center. She went back to school to obtain her Master of Arts degree in College and University Administration. She attended Michigan State University. After graduating with a MA degree, Suzan returned to Eastern Michigan University to work as a professional administrator for three years. She then found employment at the University of Nevada Reno.

Unfortunately her father passed away shortly before she moved to Reno. During this period of her life she took time to evaluate her values and goals. She had always dreamt of owning a bed and breakfast. After extensive reflection, she was convinced that she need not wait to pursue what was most important in her life. Stepping out on faith and the wings of many prayers, Suzan retired from University Administration at the youthful age of twenty-nine and began seeking her purpose in life.

Her experiences were leading her on a life transformation that would change her destiny. She had been saving money and wanted to invest in a bed and breakfast upon retirement. She actually started looking in Nevada when her family called her. One of her sister's, who is in real estate, called and stated, 'Suzan, I found it'. Upon visiting home, she realized that the lodge, which had been vacant for over four years, was her dream. In 1993, Suzan Anthony purchased the lodge and worked tirelessly in renovating the lodge without taking away from its integrity. With the help of family, she started moving items into the rooms. She attended estate state sales to find furniture to match the motif of the era. She started making the necessary plans needed to undertake such an elaborate project.

She stated in her own words that, *"The lodge was ideal for my needs and resources. It was large enough to make a living of, but small enough that I could do it myself. In the beginning there was a sister who was also interested in the bed and breakfast business, and she agreed to invest and become my partner. Being from a close family, I also had a brother who expressed an interest in my return home. He also agreed to invest and provide labor for the renovation process. My sister quickly lost interest due to other life circumstances and the fact that the lodge seemed to be a virtual 'money pit.' Tension increased as I felt very alone and my two siblings felt their finances bleed."*

The winter of 1994 was a severe one. The temperatures hovered at thirty below zero for two weeks. One night approximately, two weeks into living in the massive lodge, the furnace exploded. The fuel had become thick and old, resulting in the octopus arms of the vintage furnace dangling, as smoke bellowed. She braved the cold weather in an effort to maintain heat but the gallant old furnace had given up the ghost. Plus on occasion, in the middle of the night, Suzan thought she heard things, 'go bump in the night', leading to more frustration and worry.

Being single, she lived alone with only her two dogs for company, besides her very supportive family who visited her and offered her encouragement. Yet Suzan was determined to return the Pine Lodge to original splendor. Nothing would deter her from her lifelong dream, so the refurbishment continued.

Approximately ten months into renovations Suzan's sister called her attention to an ad in the paper regarding someone looking for a place to lodge and cross-country ski. Thinking that she could provide the lodging and that they could possibly ski down the road at Garland, she answered the ad enthusiastically. The author of the ad, Douglas James Stiles, was disappointed that she had misunderstood the advertisement. He was looking for a lodge that he could lease for the winter and run a cross-country ski business out of. Both disregarded the entire conversation, apologized for the misunderstanding, and hung up the phone, each going about their own personal business.

Approximately two weeks later Doug called Suzan again. He suggested that perhaps they could work together. Susan stated that, *"Since I already had the lodge and he intended to invest in a grooming machine along with a hot tub. We met, worked out a plan, and entered into business together. Initially we charged only seven dollars a day for the skiing. Additionally I paid him five dollars per room for use of the hot tub that he installed."*

Doug and Suzan soon discovered that they had similar goals. Before long they realized that they were very compatible with similar interests and goals. Neither had been married, and besides what were the chances of love being found in the remote region of Lewiston except for destiny's call beneath the shadows of the whispering pines? The weekend work drew them closer together and before long their friendship blossomed.

Providence called and in a short time they fell in love. They decided to get engaged. That magic moment came when Doug arrived at the lodge one Friday night after work to groom trails. Suzan stated that, *"Doug asked me to go with him and ride on the back of the groomer. It sounded like fun, so I accepted. It was a beautiful December night; snow was falling, with the night being pitch black. It was extremely cold outside as well. The only light guiding our path was that of the groomer. As we rode the trails, Doug stopped at one point and said, "I am so glad you came with me." That is all it took. Feeling my heart warm in the frigid temperatures, I replied, "Thank you. Me too." He glanced behind us and declared, "Yeah; the extra weight really helped set a better track."* Ha! Talk about the romance of the times!"

Doug and Suzan finally found the time to marry and in the month of July, 1997. With sacred vows spoken, they became man and wife. From the time she had purchased the lodge until October of 2001, Suzan worked full time managing the growing business.

Every spare moment was spent on the lodge, the grounds and cabin. They added a new roof, accomplished major renovations such as heating system, refurbishing the original integrity and look of the rustic lodge, and adding additions such as bathrooms for the seven rooms. They eliminated three guest bedrooms upstairs in order to offer adequate bathroom facilities to meet stated guidelines for a bed and breakfast. They worked tirelessly at rekindling the rustic lure of the logs and found their efforts compelling. Both invested money and work into the restoration efforts. Beautiful wood that had been covered with carpet by the previous owners was rediscovered and recovered. The kitchen was completely renovated, yet they left the authenticity of the old lodge fully intact.

Doug is a third generation master electrician who worked via the union. He rewired the lodge along with other projects needed to capture the essence of the lodge's past charm. His love for woodworking and craftsmanship led him to make vintage tables, cabinets and other items for the lodge. The couples' tireless efforts yielded the fruits of their labor and once again the old lodge received guests into their bed and breakfast. They opened the doors in December of 1994 for quests.

Then the tragic bombing on September 11, 2001, happened and the world as we knew it changed forever. Suzan decided that she needed to seek outside employment, sensing that tourism would decline. She was correct. She began working as a court reporter and continues to this day in that capacity.

To this day, Doug and Suzan Stiles preserve the history and heritage of a bygone era, when logging camps and lodges gleamed with excitement and the wonder of the indelible human spirit. They constantly seek period items to enhance the rustic heritage of the lodge. They are ever busy with refurbishment projects and preserving the integrity of their dwelling.

Historical preservations of this nature must continue, as America is only one generation away from losing its heritage, if we don't pass the torch to the rising generation. That torch is being well preserved at Pine Ridge Lodge by Suzan and Doug. It is our duty, our responsibility, and our honor to save the havens of yesterday for the future generation. The voice of the past will be potted for prosperity. Visit Pine Ridge Lodge and you will see that history and heritage is alive and well in the northern portion of Michigan. Along the way stop and embrace the other attractions offered by each state.

(Suzan, Author and Doug at Pine Ridge Lodge)

# PINE HAVEN TO PINE RIDGE

I am not sure when or why but the name of the lodge changed to Pine Ridge Lodge along the way. In my searches, I had always stopped when I typed in Pine Haven Lodge and did not think to explore other venues such as a name change. The lodge was there all along but I failed to check other addresses. Sometimes the most obvious is the difficult to see. To be totally honest with myself, my search was always at the shallow end of the pool. My half- hearted search for the lodge always came up with nothing. I now believe I was actually scared of what I might rediscover amongst the whispering pines. Now I face childhood memories which waltz with the wind. Sometimes you rediscover things about yourself when you are least prepared to do so.

(Early pictures of the lodge courtesy of the Stiles)

(Present day Pine Ridge Lodge)

(Actual table that Uncle Pug built)

# REFLECTIONS OF YESTERYEAR

I can recall when my innocence was shattered. It was upon the death of my father. I do not remember all the details, as I was only five years of age, but I am sure that it occurred in his restaurant. I remember my Uncle Tom had been cooking and the smell of Greek food permeated the air. I recall my father playing cards with a couple of men who were later identified as Italians.

My father was an immigrant from Athens, Greece, who was a stowaway on a ship. He and his brother, Thomas, were running from being an indentured servant. He came to America to find the good life and once he obtained citizenship, he continued to live in Little Greece and then on Woodrow Avenue. He spoke with a heavy accent. He discouraged me learning to speak Greek and wanted me to 'Learna the English'. He always told me that I was an American with Greek heritage. He often said for me to be proud of both but embrace America as my home. He adored the concept of America's freedom and beauty. He was proud of his citizenship. I recently discovered that he served his country, HIS America, in World War I, as a naturalized citizen. I am fiercely proud of that and the bloodline that runs in my veins rejoices in being an American.

My father washed dishes to make a living and worked his way to owning a modest restaurant. But he had a problem in that he gambled. I remember my mother crying because men came and took some furniture that my Papa lost through gambling. I have never picked up the cards due to those memories.

I was told that my mother met my father in a restaurant that he owned. She worked for him as a waitress. Their friendship blossomed into love and they were married on April 16, 1945, in Covington, Kentucky. Mother's sister, Aunt Ellie, and her husband, Uncle James Kyle, were witnesses. From the union, I was born two years later.

The memories have faded of my early years but I do recall the harrowing incident that mother never discussed with me. I was at my father's restaurant. I don't know why I was at the restaurant that night. I think mother had worked the day shift and didn't wish to be there around the men playing cards. She thought that card playing was wicked and argued with papa about it. I imagine Papa and Uncle Tom were to watch over me. My Uncle Tom was very protective of his little brown-eyed boy and was very funny. His accent was more pronounced than my fathers and he seemed to be jovial most of the time. He always tickled me and made me laugh. I couldn't understand him that often, especially when he was excited and started talking fast. He was my great entertainer and loved me dearly.

My mind has rehashed those moments in time as I once again bring to mind Uncle Tom cooking at the grill behind the counter. He loved to cook and was especially proud of his Greek dishes. I loved his cabbage rice and Christmas bread with walnuts and raisins in it. I never acquired a taste for some of the fish dishes though. Nor can I tell you the name of the dishes. That has been lost with the demise of my father and Uncle Tom.

The counter had stools in front of it for the customers. For some reason I remember that they were red. The restaurant had a few tables with red and white checkered table cloths. Uncle Tom seemed to always be behind the counter cooking. My papa usually sat in the back of the room with his gambling friends. The smoke was dense from the cigars, cigarettes, and the voices were always loud. Rarely did they speak in English unless the Italians came to play cards. That was always a big deal. I think it was a point of honor for whichever side won the pot at the end of the night. It was a rivalry that escalated.

I was playing marbles in a corner when a loud crack got my attention. I saw my uncle run to me and then he pushed me to the floor covering me with his body. I did not see my papa. Other people in the restaurant either dropped to the floor or ran out of the door. I remember being frightened and I cried out from being terrified. Some people were yelling in a language I did not understand. Then, after what seemed an eternity, I felt someone lift me up and took me to a black car where my mother was waiting. The driver talked calmly trying to sooth my mother and me. We left the city and I went to sleep in my mother's arms. I never saw the apartment where we lived again or, to the best of my knowledge, any of the belongings.

The next morning I was awakened in unfamiliar surroundings. I was lying in a bed made of logs and was in an upstairs bedroom. The room had a window and the walls were also made of logs stained and the chinking was painted a bright white. It was quite lovely. Later I discovered the name of the place was Pine Haven Lodge. My mother smiled and looked down upon me. She wore a look on her face of glum. A man was standing behind her. I recognized him as the same man who pulled me from under my Uncle Tom's body. I later learned that his name was Morris 'Smitty' Smith. I knew him from the restaurant.

We went downstairs and I was introduced to my 'Uncle Pug' and 'Aunt Mabel'. They were Smitty's parents. I noted the gentleness in Aunt Mabel's eyes and instantly felt comfortable around her. Uncle Pug had a demeanor of roughness but I soon discovered that it was image he projected in an effort to conceal a tender heart.

I remember my mother saying this was going to be our new home. I asked about papa but received no reply. Then Aunt Mabel asked me if I wanted ice cream. She knew how to win this child's heart. Mother never talked of that night when Papa died from that day forward. In fact, mother never mentioned my father again. All my questions fell on mute ears. She carried her secrets to the grave. The things I learned were from listening to my uncles' talk when they did not think I was paying attention and others around me privy to my past.

Aunt Mabel became my greatest champion and companion. She believed in me when I didn't believe in myself. She was protective and gentle. She always encouraged me to learn new things and never once criticized my wayward ways. She always showed me the error of my thinking or behavior by allowing me to think through the problem and then drawing a conclusion. She would ask me what I had done wrong, how could I correct the problem and what could I do the next time. She always told me that we were all human and made mistakes. She said that God was the only thing perfect and we must accept the fact that we will make judgment errors. It was how we dealt with them afterwards that made all the difference. I used those sacred principles in my classroom and life. She was my mentor and friend. She became my grandmother that I never knew. She gently insisted that I call her Auntie instead of Granny. Now that I have a few years on me, I understand her reasoning.

(Aunt Mabel, Suzie, and Uncle Pug-taken January 1959)

# CABIN IN THE PINES

(Author's boyhood home)

It was love at first sight. I had never seen so much yard and such huge pine trees in my short life. I could see the sky without building intruding upon the view! There in the breach in the pines was a beautiful little log cabin. I remember walking down to the log cabin at the foot of the hill with wide-eyed wonder. The cabin was nestled beneath the protruding ridge which housed Pine Haven Lodge. In fact the lodge overlooked it, as if it was a mother hen watching over her little chick. The cabin and the location was everything I had ever dreamed. The 'long house' cabin was surrounded with pines stretching towards the heavens. Its memory has never faded with time and its roots have been buried deep within my heart.

Prior to reaching the cabin, there was a workshop filled with two tractors, a toboggan, tools, and other items so tempting for an inquisitive child. I definitely fell in that category. The workshop was where Uncle Pug and Smitty applied their wood-working crafts. It had three windows on the southern side and a big sliding door facing the east. I was always leery of walking past that shadowy building at the edge of night or after dark. I was only allowed to go in the workshop with an adult to supervise me because of all the tools and equipment it contained. Rarely did I ever go up to the second floor.

(Refurbished workshop)

An earthen food cellar was a few yards from the side door of the cabin facing the lodge. When I faced the front of the cabin, I noted an apple tree on the right. I enjoyed many of its fruit, though I was told not to eat so many green apples, but I was a stubborn youth. It was there that I learned of the meaning of green apple quick step. The green apples reminded me of how I got my nickname of Butch. It too involved apples.

# BUTCHA THE BULLDOG

(Author and his mother prior to becoming Butch)

When I lived in Detroit, Michigan, with my mother and father, we lived in an apartment building. I think the name of the area where we lived was Woodrow Avenue. It was shared by other Greek families and some Italians. I recall the term Little Greece as well. The yard had a fence dividing it in two. It was drilled into my head that I was to stay in my side of the yard.

The other side of the yard had an apple tree. It must have been late summer, for apples were ripening and a couple fell to the ground. I am not sure how old I was but I must have known what an apple was. A lady who was called 'Aunt Pearlie' was watching me from the second floor balcony. I took a bite of the apple and it was good. Now the fence was not very tall and I must have thought the apples on the other side must taste better than the one I had. To Aunt Pearlie's horror, I climbed over the fence.

No sooner had I done so than a 'bulldog' came from the first floor apartment of what I assume was an Italian family because I couldn't understand a word he said. The bulldog in reality was a small bull terrier. It came running at me with full force and latched a hold of my leg. I let out a horrendous scream. Then I felt my leg bleeding and my temper kicked in with full vengeance. I bent down and locked my teeth on that dog's ear. It let go and started yipping with complete abandonment of the kill. That is when I heard the unknown dialogue coming from the first floor apartment.

A man came out of the apartment with a broom. He saw the ghastly sight and started yelling, "You killa my dog" and proceeded to come at me with a broom, as I refused to let go of the dog's ear.

It was then that I saw my robust 'aunt' come charging down the sidewalk with her broom in hand. By then the man was trying to shove me away from his dog with his broom. My aunt sailed over the fence like an Olympic hurdler, started yelling, "You killa my boy" and the legendary duel of brooms began. I had no doubt that my aunt would be the victor and once the man made a hasty retreat, one swift slap on the posterior from dear ole auntie persuaded me to let go of the terrified terrier. The poor little pooch ran to his master vowing never to bite again. The dog's name was, "Butcha the bulldog". So the legend was born. Much to my displeasure, the name stuck. I imagine that it was due to my stubborn streak I allegedly possess.

Aunt Mabel often spoke of that incident and I wondered how she was informed of my youth. One of her little jokes with me was to say, *"I don't need a guard dog because I have my little Butch with me."* She used to joke with me and say that all though I growled on occasion, rarely barked and never bit. I took that to heart and found in my mind's eye to be the guardian of Pine Haven Lodge.

# THE SECRETS IN THE SHADOWS

Just past the apple tree by the north side of the cabin was an old dilapidated trailer. Later I discovered it filled with mysteries and material such as old military uniforms, ribbons, and costume jewelry. It also contained several letters in boxes. I wish I had read them, as I am sure they contained information about my new family.

A few yards past the trailer, in the direction of the driveway (east), was an old sawmill with slabs piled about six feet high. There was also a shed where lumber was dried for future use. The mill must have been used to saw the logs for the construction of not only the lodge but also the cabin. The mill provided me many hours of imaginings as I pretended to be a lumberjack. I would act like I was cutting logs at the mill for customers and would get paid a dollar a log. I made an imaginary fortune working that old sawmill.

There was an old panel wagon truck sitting under the pines and a hitching post was in front of the road to prevent vehicles from approaching any farther into the yard. The panel wagon served as my ambulance service. It had two doors on the back that would swing open to reveal my make believe ambulance bed. I would get behind the wheel and race to the aid of someone trapped in a cave, forest fire, or who had broken through the ice while fishing. I also used it as a camping ground during the rain. I would put my quilts in the back of it and usually be lulled to sleep by the sound of the raindrops on the roof. Smitty also owned an old black Nash Rambler. He hardly ever drove it, preferring to drive his black Chevrolet back and forth to town. I never thought of it before but all three of his vehicles were black.

During my initial inspection of the grounds, I also noted a small outhouse behind the cabin. It was about one hundred feet from entrance to the residence. I soon learned that the privy was for us. My mother always kept it exceptionally clean. Once a month she washed it down with Clorox and then put something in the hole that smelled like pine. She had a flashlight by the door in case of 'emergencies' at night and an umbrella in case of rain. She always kept an umbrella and flashlight by the door. If I was in the little house out back and it rained, I would have an umbrella. She took newspapers and lined it in an effort to keep out the wind. The 'wallpaper' didn't seem to help much during those cold Michigan winters. The wintry wind and snow during the wintry weather motivated me in hurrying with my 'duties'.

The cabin seemed huge to me. It had an area boxed in where you took your shoes off and hung up your coat. This is where mother hung the umbrella and flashlight along with other outdoor essentials. I imagined the small room was for the purpose of saving heat in the winter and not fanning the door in the summer. It worked wonders in keeping those pesky black flies, mosquitoes, ticks, and gnats out of the house. Mother told me to swat my clothes and remove my shoes before entering the inside door of the cabin just in case 'pests' were clinging to me. I always dreaded the 'ghosts' in June and July. 'Ghosts' were the term used to describe the grouping of male gnats. Those gnats would swarm in big black spheres and you could see them coming for you. If one got in your eyes they would sting like crazy.

(Inside the cabin)

Upon entering the cabin, Uncle Pug started showing us all the amenities. The kitchen was immediately to the right, with a small gas stove and refrigerator. The stove was next to the door and the refrigerator was on the outside wall away from the driveway. The walls had a few cabinets but I don't believe they were fastened to them. There was a kitchen table with chairs next to the window (the table set between the two windows) and you could look out to see the fire lane or driveway. Mother spent many hours sitting in the chair watching me play in the yard.

On the farthest wall, from the front of the cabin, was a beautiful wooden dining room hutch with a large mirror. It was dark wood. It had a couple of shelves on it and mother said that is where she would put her glass pheasants. The living room had a black leather couch with wooden arms and a rocking chair that we called a 'sitting chair'. I would wear that chair out, as I pretended to be on stage coach running from the men in black hats, praying that the Lone Ranger would come to my rescue. Soon I would be transformed into that masked man, charging to the top of the wood pile on my trusty steed with a "Hi Oh Silver Away"!

The old couch was my jungle. The pillows were transformed into panthers that would attack this young lion, which would have to protect his territory. The panther pillows would be tossed high into the air until they caught the attention of the animal tamer. Her voice would give the lion warning that it was time to go back into his cage. The dreaded, "David Philip, did you hear me, I said now," would be bellowed with the roar of a lioness and I knew that the game had ended for another day. But, unbeknownst to her, the lion would sleep only for a little while before going back on the hunt.

Walking past the couch was the only bedroom. There were a couple of windows and the side door with a screen on it. The inner wall separating the bedroom from the living area was made of logs and didn't have a door. Later I found out that the wall was added after the cabin was constructed to afford privacy for the Smiths. The room smelled of pine and moss with a hint of mildew from lack of ventilation. To my delight mother said we would put our twin beds with the night stand and put a dresser between the beds. Someday we might even get bunk beds so, if I had company, they would have a place to sleep instead of on the couch.

My twin bed has golden memories of yesteryear. On those rainy days, wintry evening, or boring nights, I would take the ironing board and turn it on top of the bed. I would then get a sheet for a sail and put it over the legs of the ironing board. Soon I would drift away into the wondrous world of 'Adventure Land' and sail the open seas. The twin bed mattress would yield to my bidding, making it a perfect ocean. I fought the pirates and I rescued damsels in distress on that mighty vessel. I always envisioned being the All-American good guy in the white hat.

Another sweet memory that floods my soul was the morning light permeating into the window each morning greeting me with a kiss from its vibrating waves. The rays of sun danced on my bed and its warmth rejuvenated my being. In the summer I placed the fan next to the window and the blades drew the cool night air into the room. I loved to feel the air cascade over my body and soon moved the fan closer to my bed. Finally it touched the bed and vibrated me to sleep. The motion and the air blowing over the covers soon lulled me to sleep. In the winter, the fan was placed close to the stove and the warm air was distributed throughout the cabin. By morning I found my head buried under the covers in an effort to stay warm, as mother always turned the thermostat down in an effort to conserve fuel.

(Wall separating bedroom from living quarters)

When they took me outside and said this was my yard, my heart leaped with joy. No longer was I confined to a small fenced in yard surrounded by concrete but I had the wilderness to explore. Both front and back yards were huge and filled with the smell of pine trees and a hint of apples. The woods were alive with large fern, some of them three feet in diameter. The white bark of the aspens beautifully distinguished and contrasted the black pines. The red and golden oak stretched their branches toward the heaven and looked down at mortal man with pity. They bowed to no man and were only subjected to God and the sound of the chain saw.

With all the beauty and glory of God's creations, there was one location that was the apex of perfection. It was the whispering pines that fascinated me the most. Nestled between the cabin and Michigan 489 was a small glen with an old grove of trees which sheltered it from any potential intruders. A cedar tree was amongst the mix of pines and I noted that it always waltzed with the wind. The ferns hugged the earth and if I decided to disappear, I would simply lie down amongst them and be out of sight. This special place became my Mecca and it was there that I prayed when I needed to feel the presence of God. The pines never failed me, as they lifted up my childish petitions towards heaven. It seemed that in the shadow of the whispering pines I found such solace in the call of the wind.

Leaning against one of the majestic trees and looking straight up, I immediately envisioned a tree house in my new safe haven. I began making youthful plans, even at such a young age, to secure the land via my observation tower! In my youth all the world laid at my feet to do my bidding. This would be my domain for six years.

I looked at Smitty, Aunt Mabel, Uncle Pug, and mother. They smiled and nodded for me to go and play. Even at such a youthful age, I felt such a sense of overwhelming freedom. That feeling has never abandoned me. Eureka, from concrete to grass! No more noisy vehicles on the busy streets of a city. No longer would I hear the siren of a fire truck or a police car. There was no worry of crime or violence. Mother never once locked the door at night and always said we were safe and was being protected by the lodge's silhouette. I came to realize that well-being is a state of mind that was afforded nurturing by the happiness of your surroundings.

On that day I said so long to the hustle and bustle of street life. My new world would be filled with the wonders of nature, the regained innocence of youth and of course, the silence and solitude of the mighty pines. My heart soared with the eagles. I was finally safe at home and my heart briefly settled from that recent troubling moment in time, as I realized this was to be my new residence.

# THE ROOT CELLAR ESCAPADE

I can't recollect the first time I met him but it must have been at my little one room school at Red Oak. His name was Danny Johns. He was dark skinned, black hair, a tad overweight but not heavy and very stout built. He was a couple of inches taller than me. He liked me from the start and I reciprocated the friendship.

Starting around the third grade, my friend, Danny Johns, would often ride his bike from his house to visit me at our cabin. He only lived a couple of miles away from me and he had the grand collie known as Zip ever present at his side. We three (and later four with Frosty) became inseparable.

The root cellar was a place we liked to climb on top of and pretend it was our castle. It was earthen with a small chimney hole or air hole at the very top. It protruded from the ground approximately eight feet and the walkway led to the cellar door. Inside it had poles, much like the ones in the workshop holding up the roof. It was always damp and dark in the 'hole'.

One day we became curious as to why it was always locked and decided to peep through the smoke hole to see what was in it. After trying to look, we decided we could get a better view if we pulled the pipe out of the ground. Sure enough the view yielded quantities of canned goods.

Danny spotted a jar with red objects and we determined it must be strawberries. We decided that I would be lowered down into the vault, get a jar and then cover up our newly created doorway. We excavated the hole until I could squeeze through and Danny lowered me down by my feet. To my dismay, about half way down his hold on my legs slipped and I plummeted to the floor. Hurting only my pride, I dusted myself off and tossed Dan the 'strawberries'. They looked rotten anyway. My senses detected the smell of mold and mildew. The dirt that I had eaten when I landed also added to my sense of awareness. Where was a flashlight when I needed one? The walls seemed to close in upon me and I was almost certain that I saw a glow in the corner from the reflection of a wild beast. Time to leave!

Then it dawned on me that I had no way out of the darkened dungeon. I started panicking. Mother would skin me alive, and I couldn't imagine what Uncle Pug would do. I hollered for Dan to get a rope and I waited while imagining all types of creations crawling along the floor.

It seemed like hours but then I heard Danny returning. To my alarm the root cellar door rattled and slowly opened with an eerie squeaking noise. I just knew it was Uncle Pug. The light shined on an angel like figure which was to be revealed as my Aunt Mabel. She had been watching our mischief from the lodge's kitchen window and when she saw me disappear, she came running down the hill. She tried to act mad but I could see the relief on her face.

The shadow lurking behind her though was unmistakable. Mother was standing there with a glare that only a disgruntled mother possesses. Aunt Mabel checked me out and said we had to be more careful then said something to my mother as she handed her the 'strawberries'. For some reason, mom turned and went inside after confining Danny and I to the perimeters of her vision. She told us to play until she rang the bell for dinner. We accepted our 'punishment' with joy and relief.

We soon forgot about the episode and played on the wood pile, rode the hitching post railing, and climbed the tree to our make-shift tree house that was under construction. We chased the squirrels with pine cones that protested our intrusion. We hid amongst the fern in an effort to see a deer or other wildlife. All was right with the world.

Mother rang the bell for dinner and we dropped what we were doing in order to 'fill our tanks'. Upon entering the cabin, I noted that Uncle Pug, Aunt Mabel, Smitty, Mr. and Mrs. Johns were going to join us for supper. Since we had a small table for three, Danny and I thought we would be eating outside. To our surprise the adults stood beside us as mom fixed our plates with mashed potatoes, bologna sandwiches, and a heaping helping of soup. We were told to offer the blessing and then to dig into our food. We complied to their wishes and before long Danny and I had forgotten the adults behind and beside us. We washed the food down with 'sweet milk'.

I don't remember the dinner topic or if the adults ate with us but I do recall the dessert. In fact, it was before the first bite that we realized we were busted. The dessert was round and slimy looking. They appeared to be yucky. They didn't look a thing like strawberries. We were told to enjoy and we gathered from the tone that it was not a request. We dug into the slippery slimy dessert with well-founded reservations. I gagged as the morsel entered my mouth but knew better than to complain. Slowly we finished our delicacy and looked up at the prying eyes of six adults.

They asked us how we liked our 'strawberries' and we of course stated we loved them. Well since we liked the strawberries so much, they decided on giving us an additional treat, and then filled our bowl with yet another heaping helping of the dreaded vegetable I cannot stomach to this day: BEETS! From that day forward we avoided the shadow of the earthen root cellar. Lesson learned.

# SMITTY

Morris A. 'Uncle Pug' Smith son's name was Morris A. Smith Jr. We all called him Smitty and sometimes Uncle Pug called him Junior. I always thought he was named after his father. He was such a kind man and he always wore a smile. He was very tall, long, thin, and lanky. His face was slender and his hair was retreating. He walked slinging his arms, bouncing along, and whistling. I loved to hear his crisp whistle and the musical melody he was able to recreate as a whistler. He could imitate different bird calls and they would sometimes answer him. He always wore a ball cap and was a diehard Detroit Lions and Tigers fan.

His glasses were thick, his features plain, but his demeanor always brightened my day. I can still hear his favorite sayings. He would always say 'for crying in the sink' when something went wrong and 'for goodness sake' if something pleased him. 'Holy cow' was an expression of excitement and wonder. 'For Pete's sake' could be good or bad pending on the tone of his voice. On occasion he would use the phrase, 'Son of a gun' but not once did I ever hear him curse or raise his voice in any manner. He did smoke, as did my mother, but I do not recall them ever smoking in the car or in the house. Even in winter, mother would step out to smoke those terrible cigarettes that I loathed. I used to fantasize about raiding stores and burning all the tobacco products so they could never smoke again. I think it made me determined never to smoke or chew.

Smitty always was glad to see me and let me know it by his actions. On several occasions he would swing me around in a circle and I would giggle with delight. He would often ask me how his 'favorite boy' was doing and I would beam. His personality revolved around the positive. I knew him from the restaurant that my father owned. He was always eating there. I believe he worked in a factory while in Detroit, Michigan. He was the man who rescued me on that terrible night when darkness intruded upon my youth.

One of my favorite memories of Smitty was when he would take me to Mio. It was nestled in a valley next to the mighty Au Sable River. The little villa was founded in 1881, and was named after one of the town's founders. She was called Mioe. Somewhere down the line, when the post office was named after her, they lost the letter e.

Located in the city was a beautiful shrine honoring God that I didn't fully understand but knew it was important. It had a cross, a fountain, a statue of Jesus and of Mary. The shrine was made of rocks and stood several feet high. It was probably three stories tall. It looked like a sky scraper to me. You could even walk inside of it. Inside the cave-like structure were statues and pictures. Even at my age, I knew it was a holy place and to enter into it, one must do so with reverence. The church next to it was called, The Lady of the Woods.

(Shrine as it looks today)

On occasion, there was a carnival on the outskirts of the city. I vividly recall all the rides, cotton candy, and prizes that Smitty won for me. He had quite an arm on him when it came to knocking bottles over with a ball. Mio also possessed the most delicious ice cream shop. It was there that I tasted my first milkshake. Near the town, the grand AuSable was dammed up and made what I thought was a lake. We went up there from time to time and had a picnic. The pond was gorgeous. It was known as Mio Dam Pond.

Every Wednesday, Smitty would come down to the cabin after work and make his "world famous and internationally known" spaghetti and meat balls. The meat balls looked like they weighed a pound a piece and he had his own special recipe for the sauce. I would drool in anticipation of the meal. Along with that delicacy he would create delicious homemade chocolate shakes. I can still feel my belly pushing against my belt from gorging myself.

The first time I visited Lewiston, Michigan, was alone with Smitty. He had told me of a tree with branches that made a W. I couldn't imagine it. Upon reaching the outskirts of town, I was amazed at what I saw. The reason I remember Lewiston, Michigan, so vividly is because of the W tree in front of a laundry mat. The tree had branches that actually formed a W. Folks around the area knew exactly where you were talking about when you mentioned the W tree of Lewiston. God's wonders was there spelled out by that unique "letter-shaped" tree.

I think the other thing that impressed my youthful mind and left a lasting impression was the people who worked at the Laundromat. They looked different than most people of the area and though time has dimmed my intellect, I believe they were of oriental ancestry. To be honest I was a little scared of the man but the nice lady won my heart on our first visit. She smiled at me and then went in the back area. Upon her return she held in her hand a big sucker and then gave it to me. I was shy at first but took the sucker. I said a weak thank you to the nice lady avoiding eye contact. I was reminded to speak up and always be polite to my elders. I said it again but this time louder. I noted her oval shaped eyes and her complexion. I thought she was so beautiful and she had long flowing hair fixed in a different manner than I had ever seen. I do believe that may have been my first love.

Smitty took his work-uniforms into Lewiston to have them cleaned on occasion. I made several trips with him but always had an ulterior motive in doing so. I believe it was for the love of the lady and the love of suckers. Upon reflection, I don't recall having a washing machine. I do remember mother washing clothes in the kitchen sink and occasionally in my 'bath tub'. We didn't have many clothes and kept everything we had in a five-drawer dresser. We did not have a closet. On pretty days, mother would hang the clothes outside and if it rained or was cold, she would hang them indoors. On occasion she would dry them by the gas heating stove or kitchen stove.

In my later years I know we went up to the lodge to wash items but don't remember anything about the details of doing the laundry. Sometimes the small things linger in our minds and then there are times that everyday items leave without a trace of acknowledging their existence.

Lewiston was built between two beautiful lakes, correctly named Twin Lakes. One of the lakes was on the east side of town and the other on the west. One was larger than the other but I am not sure which one. I loved going there. You could walk to the waterfront from downtown Lewiston and enjoy the beach. I thought the lakes were massive.

(Twin Lake Beach within a short walking distance of Lewiston, Michigan)

There was an old pine tree that grew out from the bank and leaned into the water. That was my favorite spot on the beach and I loved climbing across the tree thinking of the impending dangers lurking below the surface. I loved lying beneath its branches hiding from the sun and the other swimmers. There were so many ponds and lakes in the region that I can't recall them all. There was an old store on the corner and I used to get candy and soda pop there. Other than that, I only recall that Smitty worked in the town sometimes and there was a soda shop in town.

The settlement known as Lewiston reminded me of an old west town in its design, with wide streets and friendly people. It was named after a man by the name of Lewis Jenson who owned a Lumber Company. It was founded in 1891.

I often fancied myself at high noon walking down Main Street with my silver handled pistols holstered, facing the dreaded gang of outlaws, which infested the fair town. My mission was to rid the streets once and for all of those scoundrels. I could hear the escalades of the people shouting and showering my bullet ridden body with gifts. It always seemed that it was always the magical ice cream man' mystical remedy that would nurture me back to health. I was made High Sheriff and the town grew in prosperity under my watchful eye.

Grayling, Michigan, was another city that I vividly recall. It had a huge fish hatchery and was named after a fish that no longer lives in the waters of the area. I also thought there was a military base close by. I saw military men and copied the way they walked. I even learned to salute. Also a few of the downtown buildings were brightly painted and Fred Bear had his famous archery factory and museum there. He gave us a personal tour of the facilities once and we visited his museum on numerous occasions.

There was a state park close to Grayling that was the largest park in the Lower Peninsula. It was called Hartwick State Park and was covered with beautiful white pines. It had a logging camp theme and there was a set of red wagon wheels that I thought was huge. I had a picture taken there with me pointing at the wheels. We must have visited the park in the fall because the colors were unbelievable. I felt like Paul Bunyan as I surveyed the trees needing to be harvested for winter quarters.

Almost every evening we would go for a walk down the road towards the "Reeds", which is really known as Wright Creek. Funny, I was never scared when Smitty went walking with me. Sometimes we would drive on the fire lanes. We would end up at Muskrat Lake, Glen Lake, Pickerel Lake, Tee Lake, Au Sable River, Little Bear Lake, the other cabins around the lodge, or some other unknown destinations.

One evening we were at Muskrat Lake fishing. The fish were not biting so we started wading. We rolled up our breeches and took off our shoes. I can still feel the mud between my toes and the smell of the stagnate water. The water was up around my knees and on occasion reached my waist. The mosquitoes and gnats were having a field day. In order to dampen their spirits, I splashed water on my face and around my bare arms. One look from mother made me aware that

I could splash myself but not her or Smitty. Funny what a glance can say!

It seems like we waded all the way across that lake but I am sure it must have been deeper than that. All I know is that my skin was wrinkled from staying in the water so long and when we got home I had to take a bath to get rid of the yuck between my toes and toenails. It must have been an inlet because on my visit to the lake in July of 2010, I realized that I had been mistaken about the size and depth of the lake. The park was closed due to some unknown reason to me, but never-the-less, I walked the very path of my childhood.

I saw prints of animals, which in my mind, are the descendants of the ones I saw as a youth. I heard the meadow lark calling his mate. The jays chattered amongst the trees and were up to their usual mischief. The squirrels teased me, as they circled the tree in a game of hide and seek. The minnows welcomed me and the elusive bluegill darted shyly in the waters. The pines recognized me and bowed in acknowledgement of a time long ago. The wind carried the voices of yesterday to me. The ferns invited me to come and walk with them in yet another adventure, likened unto my youth. Chills ran over my body and tears of gratitude once again fell unabated from my eyes. The memories sustained me then as it did in my youth.

# THE FIRE LANE BEAR

One excursion took us down the fire lane. We parked our car in a wide place, avoiding the thick sand where we might have gotten stuck. As we leisurely walked along the road, I looked up in the tree line and noted two dark objects amongst the pines. Upon closer observation, I realized that I had spotted two small cubs. They were clinging to the tree. They were so cute looking down at us. I thought they would make great pets for us and our school. The babies might even belong to Smokey. I informed Smitty, Mom, and my friend, Danny Johns, with great excitement about my discovery. When Smitty spotted them, he looked in all directions and motioned for us to be still and not to speak so the cubs wouldn't be alarmed. Smitty softly stated that where there were young cubs, the mother would be nearby and she would be very protective of her babies. We were immediately told to walk gradually away from the area but do not run or walk fast. Smitty stayed behind, walking slowly, watching for the mother bear. Once we were all back in the car, the mother bear slowly meandered down the narrow road. She stopped on occasion to check on her cubs and to see if there was a threat. I saw the look of relief on mother and Smitty's face. Later I came to appreciate the value of that lesson. Respect for the wonders of nature when in her garden is the first rule of being outdoors.

# WHEN ENCOUNTERING A BLACK BEAR

The Northern Michigan area in which I lived was notorious for black bears and wild turkeys. A little sleepy villa known as Curran, Michigan, even boasted that their city was the black bear capital of Michigan. As the eagle flies, the town was only twenty or so miles away from where we lived. It stands to reason that bears meandered and migrated into different areas and no doubt was in my secluded neck of the woods. The town of Fairview, Michigan, was called the wild turkey capitol of the world. Atlanta was known as the elk capital of Michigan. With that much game it makes perfect sense that predators roamed the land and followed the seasonal food source. Every time I turned around I was reminded to be careful when I was in the woods and to take the dogs with me.

One day Smitty read a story to me from a local newspaper about a child being snatched up by a bear. A neighbor, who witnessed the incident, ran out and punched the bear right smack dab in the nose. The Good Samaritan's action surprised the bear so that he immediately dropped the child. Smitty looked at me over his glasses and stated that I should never try that, for it would probably provoke the bear even more.

He went on to instruct me on what to do if I ever encountered a bear in the woods. The best medicine was prevention. He told me about an old Indian trick where you wore bells on your ankle so that you don't startle the bear. The bear would hear you coming due to the jingle and not be surprised. He paused just a second then added that it wasn't a dinner bell but the bell let them know you were in the area. He laughed at his wisecrack. I didn't think it funny at all.

He said to never run but slowly back off and make myself as big as possible. Watch out for cubs in trees and never get between a sow bear and her cubs. She was very protective of them. Listen to the sounds while in the forest. Every noise or lack of it has a purpose. When you see a bear, he may smack his jaws trying to intimidate you. Sometimes this means the bear was upset or nervous. He also stated that if the bear gave a bluff charge, stand your ground and yell with a deep voice, making yourself as large as possible.

Finally he said if it continues to charge, quickly bend over, grab your ankles with your hands, and quickly kiss your butt goodbye. He roared with delight at my wide-eyed wonder. He had a good sense of humor, and I got the point though I was not amused. Respect the bear and all the animals in the forest, for you are in their home. I guess his methods must have worked because the only bears I ever saw were cubs in a tree and one dead bear beside the road.

# THE PIANO, POTS, AND PANS CHOIR

The only other incident I can summon up from my memory which involved a bear was when Uncle Pug, Aunt Mabel, and mother took me to a special place. I don't remember where Smitty was but I think he was working. Uncle Pug loved the logging history and someone had told him of an old abandoned logging camp somewhere around Mio, I believe. It could have even been in McKinley, Fairview, or Comins, Michigan, area. All I know is that he decided to take us on a trip to see the old logging community. Uncle Pug talked about it as we traveled to see it. The camp had been built in the early turn of the century and consisted of a make-shift sawmill, long houses, and a mess hall. He stated that it was very rough and run down but he wanted to take pictures of it.

We made it to the place where it was located and parked the car. We had to walk into the forest and the undergrowth indicated that the area had been logged years ago. We walked along a crystal blue stream and I could not help but notice the fish. I wished I had brought my fishing pole to wreak havoc on those unsuspecting morsels. Today they would be spared, for the pathfinder had to lead his small party to the safety of the logging camp.

Uncle Pug continued walking and finally we arrived at the old camp site with dilapidated buildings. I counted four long house cabins and on a small ridge stood the remnants of a mess hall. The mill itself was beyond recognition by my green horn eyes but Uncle Pug seemed delighted to find the saw blade and an old two handle saw that he added to his collection in the workshop. He was quite gifted in wood working. Uncle Pug directed our focus to the mess hall and stated that he wanted to go in and look around. As we walked, he noted bear tracks and told us to stay close and watch for any old sows that might be in the area.

We walked to the mess hall and went inside. The windows had broken glass remnants and the smell inside the hall was that of mold and mildew. The curtains were faded and torn. I was impressed to see that the curtain rods were nothing more than a pine limb. Several items were scattered on the floor, such as a broken glass, dishes, papers, and metal pans that were now unusable. There were a few antlers on a poorly constructed mantle and a mirror that had faded with time. The dust was over everything, even the floor. Uncle Pug called us over and noted the bear signs in the mess hall. He said they were fresh and that we needed to leave. At that point there was a noise outside and at first I thought it was a buck rubbing his antlers against the logs. Uncle Pug didn't seem to agree.

He closed the door hurriedly and in the corner was a broken down piano, much out of tune from years of abandonment and neglect. He went straight to it and told us to gather the pots and pans off the floor. We did and then he said on his signal, to begin beating them together while shouting. As soon as we complied with his demands, Uncle Pug started banging on the piano as loud as he could and crooned with all the ability of Frank Sinatra. Whatever was out there took off with a snort and after thinking about it all these years, I would have too! Imagine the noise being created from within a building that had been silent for over fifty years. I could see in my mind's eye a great exodus of not only bear, but also anything with legs or creatures able to crawl, hop, and jump to escape the unearthly noises being generated from the pot, pan, and piano choir.

As we left, Uncle Pug looked at the signs left behind and stated he was confident it was a bear. He then looked at us and with a wink that was infrequent with his character stated that the animals of the woods would be talking about this day for generations to come. I wanted to take my pot lid with me but was told to leave it or the bear would follow us home to reclaim its prize. I quickly dropped it along the trail. Years later I saw a Disney movie where the animals were singing and I thought they probably got the idea from the pots and pans choir.

# SUZIE AND FROSTY

(Frosty, the Wonder Dog)

The Smith's had a beautiful black, white, and brown collie that they called Suzie. Her back was black, chest white and she had a white ring around her neck. Suzie had brown patches around her eyes with a white strip on her nose that ran up and down her face. She appeared to be wearing socks of white and brown on her feet. She was such an adorable dog. She was such a gentle creature and so friendly. Suzie would waddle to me whenever I was up at the lodge. She lived inside the lodge but was allowed to go out whenever she wished. Whenever we were alone, I would call her Lassie though she did not resemble Lassie in the least.

I must have been seven years of age when I got my very own dog. He was a bundle of joy wrapped in pasty white fur. For some reason, whenever I looked at the pup, he seemed to smile at me. It was a reciprocating feeling and my love for him grew in leaps and bounds.

That first night, I played with my pup until it was bedtime. I placed the pup beside my bed and he protested being imprisoned by the walls of the box. Mother told me to get an alarm clock, wrap it in a towel, and put it in the box. I said to myself how crazy that sounded but knew not to question her wisdom. I placed the swaddled clock in his box and to my surprise all the whining and whimpering stopped. Amazing how smart adults could be at times.

Whenever Suzie's saw the pup the next morning, her motherly instinct kicked in. She immediately took the pup under her wing and was so gentle with the eight week old. The pup was a gift from my teacher and he was snow white with a bushy long tail. I named him Frosty due to his coloration. He was an English Retriever. I am sure he was mixed but for my purposes I imagined him as a white Lassie and I was Tim. He showed an abnormal interest in birds and would stand perfectly still with his tail straight prior to charging into the urgent flutter of wings. And there was something about that tail. The hair on his tail was elongated. He was highly intelligent. He too was very gentle in nature.

The thing I remember most of all was Frosty's love and devotion to me. If I was sitting at the kitchen table, he would be outside underneath the window. If I was in the bedroom at night, he would be at that location. When he heard my voice in the morning, he would place his front paws on the cabin's logs and look into the window, panting all the time. His tail would gyrate back and forth in a wagging contortion, gaining momentum whenever I pecked on the window. He would run to the front door in anticipation of a pat on the head or a treat. Whenever I stepped out of the cabin, he would begin the love fest of jumping, running back and forth, wiggling and on occasion bark. I had to stifle the barking, as it became annoying to all except his master. When Susie was outside with him, he didn't get so excited. Susie was a very dignified dog and it must have rubbed of on Frosty. Susie loved to come to me for pats and hugs.

The only dog he ever tried to fight was my friend, Danny Johns' dog. His dog's name was Zip. Zip was a full stock collie and reminded me so much of Lassie. He followed Danny everywhere, as did my dog, Frosty, shadowed me. They only times they would collide was when each master paid attention to the other one's pet. Whenever we would take off riding our bikes, here they would come. Frosty was only allowed to go down to the lane but Zip followed Danny everywhere, including the highway. I thought it unfair but all the adults agreed, so I was outvoted. Soon Frosty knew his perimeters and adhered to the rules.

# LUCKY

Smitty was given a full stocked cocker spaniel by someone at work. We soon discovered why. Her name was Lucky but she did not live up to that title. She was beautiful with long reddish-golden hair. Lucky was very friendly and had been an inside dog. Mother did not want her in the house so she stayed outside most of the time and would play with Suzie and Frosty.

Somewhere in her past, Lucky had acquired a taste for porcupine flesh. She would disappear for days at a time. When she came home she would be badly swollen with porcupine quills all in her mouth and nose. We would have to take her to the Veterinarian in order to save her life. Once she mended though, No matter how bad she was injured, she would go right back and kill another porcupine. There was a preponderance of porcupines in the area. In fact one big porcupine loved to chew on the logs at the cabin and we had to put pieces of metal by the door to keep them from gnawing at the end of the logs. Finally he had to be trapped and removed from the area. He was large and probably weighed around thirty-five pounds. One thing I learned is that they do not throw their quills but they are quite loud. They are nocturnal and are a large rodent.

I recall one time when that poor dog came back to the cabin with her mouth so swollen with quills. I felt so sorry for her. I was running around outside barefooted and stepped on a quill. It stuck in my big toe. I tried to pull it out but it had a barb on the end of it. Mother and Aunt Mabel took me to the doctor. He looked at it and said he would have to clip it off and let it work its way out. That scared me because in my child's mind I could see it surfing throughout my body. He clipped it, and put some disinfectant on it. Sure enough it worked its way through without too much discomfort but I remember playing it for all it was worth in terms of getting out of my household duties. For a few weeks I was excused from trash duty, mowing with that old non-motorized mower, and other chores that required walking. I still had to make my bed though.

Lucky was a sweet and loving dog but whenever she got out of her pen, she would find a way of escape and be gone a few days, only to return with those barbs deep within her mouth. It was as if the night lured her into the forest. An older man who owned the only store in the Red Oak area told Smitty that once a dog tasted porcupine meat, it couldn't be broken of killing them to eat. He said it was much like a bear to honey; simply irresistible. Finally Lucky was given away to someone else, but upon reflection, I believe she may have found another fate.

# THE LUCK OF A SKUNK

Thank goodness Frosty was different. He was a big baby and just wanted to play with the animals around the house. He joyfully chased squirrels as they scolded him from the safety of a pine tree. He was so curious, that it wasn't funny. Mother said he was the perfect complement to my curiosity. Sometimes though, curiosity can get you in trouble.

One evening we were walking up to the new cabin which was being built on the other road. The road was filled with adventure on each side, with ferns two-three foot wide and encroaching upon the latest construction project. The smell of pine permeated the air and the breeze made my heart waltz with the wind.

It was Frosty who brought me back to reality. For some reason he let out a bark and ran straight at the cabin. Out of inquisitiveness, I ran behind him encouraging his stride. I noted that Suzie lagged behind and that was not like her. She usually ran beside of her pup. Frosty reached the cabin and started immediately digging under the foundation. I thought sure he was after a rabbit. I thought I would have to build a cage to keep the rabbit contained. It would make a great addition to my animal collection.

I got closer to see what he was up to when all of a sudden a pungent odor overcame both of us. The smell was hideous. We both had been in direct line of fire from a very irritated skunk's spray. Both of us cried in agony and went running home with our tails between our legs.

Upon arriving home, mother came out of the cabin but did not have to ask why I was crying. The aroma immediately told her of the situation and my poignant condition. She instructed me to take every stitch of clothes I had on off and she prepared a tub of water for me. There I was in my birthday suit waiting for the scrub down. Mother kept scolding Frosty and told him to stay away. Now I realize why.

Mother went to the lodge and to my dismay; she came back with Aunt Mabel. Auntie apparently had experience in dealing with such an odor, for she brought a big can of tomato juice to 'treat' me with it. To my humiliation and embarrassment, she rubbed tomato juice all over me with a scrub brush. All the time she was either crying from the 'tear gas' or laughing at the pitiable scene. Mother was not any help either, due to her uncontrollable laughter. Never have I been so humiliated. Frosty didn't escape the treatment either though he was allowed to keep his fur.

# THE GREAT WHITE HUNTER

One day I decided to go hunting for grouse. I had never seen one but I heard the hunters talking about how good they were to eat. I decided to surprise mother and Aunt Mabel with a dozen or so for dinner. I got my trusty Bear Bow and quiver with the practice arrows that was given to me by Fred Bear and started out on my quest. I had to walk down the lane so mother would not see me go into the dark pine thicket. The area that I had selected was known for the thickness of its underbrush and the foliage that made walking difficult and visibility limited.

I walked quietly along the small path I claimed for my own. It actually was a deer path and I had accidently found it on a previous outing. I started picking my private patch of blueberries which was located in a small glen and eating them. There is nothing better than to find a patch of blueberries while hunting and eating those little morsels. My lips and tongue were blue by the time I finished gorging myself.

I checked high and low but there was not one animal to be seen. I saw a stump with some underbrush and decided to quietly walk to the stump and use it as a hunting base. I stepped over some brush at my feet and to my shock; a loud rustling noise took stormed out of the bushes right under my feet. I dropped my bow in one direction and took flight in the other. There was no doubt some dark hideous monster was hot on my trail. I didn't look back until I got in sight of the cabin where I once again felt safe.

I went up to the lodge and told Smitty about the creature that attacked me and he went with me to see what I had discovered. He took his trusty pocket knife but I thought sure he would need a machine gun. Whatever disarmed me was huge and vicious. Upon arriving at the scene of the attack, my bow was laying right where I threw it. As Smitty went over to pick it up, sure enough the thundering sound occurred again and then faded into the forest. He laughed and said I had succeeded in finding my quarry. I had no clue what he meant until he told me.

Indeed I had found the elusive grouse and it was the flutter of their wings that made the strange sound. I begged him not to tell Uncle Pug or the hunters at the lodge a bird scared me so bad that I threw down my trusty bow and ran like a scared rabbit. He said it would be our secret and besides, I think the noise scared him too. To the best of my knowledge, he kept his promise. Sometimes between men, secrets forge a bond that cannot be broken.

# THE BEAVER DAM

I don't know how many times I passed it but I knew what it was. I was convinced that it was a beaver dam even though I never saw one swimming in the pond. I guess I never got off my bike to look. One day when I was relaxing at the lodge with the men folk, we talked about beavers and the value that used to be placed on their pelts. I mentioned the beaver dam and Smitty said there weren't any beavers there but I knew there had to be. I wanted to prove him wrong. So I came up with a plan. I thought maybe I need to take my trusty bow and bag me a beaver. Of course the mere mention of such brought the wrath of mother upon my head for wanting to hurt one of God's creatures. So I was forbidden to take any weapon out of the house. It was time for a new plan. It seemed I was always in the process of planning bigger and better schemes.

I was determined to at least see one. I packed a snack and went to the area by myself. I guess I was about eight or nine years of age. I imagined that I would see this furry mammal swimming with its babies and slapping its tail against the water as a warning to its offspring of impending danger. I even had my trusty Kodak camera with me to capture the moment. My new plan was to show the evidence and make Smitty eat crow.

I built a small blind and laid down watching the water. I listened to the sounds of Blue Jays arguing with each other, squirrels squawking in the trees, and the rustle of the wind. Soon I found myself lulled to sleep in the pines.

I am not sure what awakened me but I knew something was close. It might have been the hoot of an owl. I looked out of my make shift blind and there it was. A nice sized beaver was within a few yards of me. The tail was not flat but I thought it must be a juvenile. I slowly reached for my Kodak and gently snapped the shutter. The noise made the beaver bolt into the water. In a moment its head came up and for the life of me the thing looked more like a big rat. I took another picture. I had the proof I needed.

I ran home and asked Mother if she would take the film to get it developed. She said once I used it all she would. So I started taking pictures of Frosty, Suzie, my shoe, and anything to use up all the film. She took the film to the store on the next grocery run. In a week we got the film back and there was my beaver in all its glory.

I decided to go up to the lodge and share my pictures not only with Smitty but the guests who were hunting or fishing on the preserve. I went in the kitchen, as was my custom. Aunt Mabel always said the front door was for guests and the back door was for family. They were a group of men gathered in the living room as I went into the den. A man by the name of Bill greeted me with his usual tussling of my hair. I liked him because he always gave me a dime when he saw me. I watched for his car when hunting season opened. He was a big burley man and once gave me a ride in his brand new Pontiac. It was the fanciest thing I had ever seen with so much chrome I had to cover my eyes to avoid the glare of the sun's reflection. That new car smell was the first I had ever experienced. I remember offering up a prayer for him when on my knees at bedtime.

I went to Smitty and told him I had proof that the dam belonged to a beaver. He looked at me and stated, "Where is your proof son?" I proudly displayed my two pictures of the beaver to Smitty. I noted a grin from ear to ear as he simply passed the pictures to the other men. They cackled. Uncle Pug looked at it and died laughing. I was puzzled about their behavior. Had they never seen a beaver before?

Aunt Mabel came in and asked what all the laughter was about. They showed her the picture. She didn't laugh though. She looked at her husband and son. Her brow wrinkled as she declared that they ought to be ashamed of themselves and asked me to go into the kitchen with her. She went to a bookshelf and got an encyclopedia. She turned the pages until she found what she was looking for. She found a picture of a beaver, pointed to it, and read about it to me. Then she showed me another picture and asked me the difference. I immediately knew the error of my ways. Aunt Mabel had saved me from a big embarrassment. The creature I had captured with my camera for all to see was not a beaver at all. It was the animal a local lake was named after: Muskrat Lake...

(Muskrat Lake-4 miles from Pine Ridge Lodge)

# FISHING FUN

Frosty was also a fishing dog, much to my displeasure. Let me explain. You see, whenever we let him go with us to the old mill pond or one of the small streams in the area, he sat on the bank quietly. As soon as we caught a brook trout or rainbow, there he went either lunging at our dangling trophy or attempted to duplicate our act by pouncing into the water with a mighty splash. He would spring into the water as the fish scurried away from his antics. The only exception to this technique was when he attempted to catch them in the strong current with his mouth. I am confident that the fish simply laughed at his efforts and easily exited without being caught. As much as I wished for him to stop doing this, he never did and needless to say, his fishing excursions with us were limited. I found it fascinating that when we didn't have our poles, Frosty never acted in that manner. Upon reflection, maybe he was simply seeking needed attention or proving that he was just as good as we were when it came to such. I believe he was correct on both counts.

# BULL HEADS

On one occasion we went to a lake. Its name has faded with age but the memory of that day still abides. I think it might have been Pickerel Lake but am not sure. Somehow Uncle Pug persuaded mother to allow me to go out on his wooden row boat and fish. Aunt Mabel and mom stayed in camp cooking while Smitty maintained the fire. He also was charged with keeping a close eye on the camp and the ladies in case an unwanted four legged friend decided to visit. He was just that way; caring and thoughtful.

I had fished on the bank before but it was always for brook or rainbow trout. My pond fishing experience had been limited to blue gill or sunfish. Never had I fished from a boat. Now here I was on a lake! My excitement was that of a child who saw his first puppy in the window of a pet store. My world expanded on that day.

That day we were fishing for a fish Uncle Pug called bull heads. I had never heard the term and was too embarrassed to ask what type of fish that they were. He rolled us out to his favorite fishing spot and cast his line in the water. I recall him instructing me on how to bait my hook for this type of fish. Within a couple of minutes I saw my line tighten. I got ready to set the hook and on my first tug, hooked a large one. He put up quite the battle. I thought it must be a monster but to my surprise when it surfaced, it was only about ten inches in length. It looked funny. I had never seen a fish with whiskers before. It looked more like a cat than a fish.

I pulled it in the boat, grabbed it like I would a blue gill and got the shock of my life. It stung me with its barbs and when I threw it down, Uncle Pug chuckled. The worst part was when I tried to take the hook out of its mouth; it bit me though I fought back the tears. Uncle Pug then informed me that a bull head was a catfish and that they bite as well as sting. Wish I had that information before I handled it.

After getting that confounded thing off the hook, I recast my line praying not to get another. Every time the line moved, I would jerk prematurely in hopes of eluding the big one. I jerked so hard on one occasion that my hook landed on Uncle Pug's hat which for some unknown reason was lying in the boat. He was busy casting and didn't see me hook it. Uncle Pug treasured his old fishing hat. He had a series of artificial baits, such as Rooster Tails, Rapala, homemade lures, sinkers, and other adornments, dangling from it. The hat must have weighed ten pounds! No wonder it wasn't on his head.

I thought if I could just get up and get it before he noticed it, he wouldn't say anything to me. As soon as I stood I realized the error of my ways.

The boat shifted and I fell to one side. With my hand I involuntarily jerked the fishing pole and off went Uncle Pug's hat right into the water. I was petrified. That was his favorite fishing hat dangling in the water on the end of my line. What if the line broke or sunk before I could reel it to the safe confines of our boat. Half mad and half tickled, he looked at me and simply said, "Boy you got a big one there and you best reel it in carefully." Fortunately for me the hat stayed afloat long enough for me to reel it in and have my hook removed from the hat by my distraught uncle. He let the fishing hat dry before he put it back on his head, though he continued to warn me about removing any flesh from his scalp with my hook. I wasn't sure if he was joking but I took careful aim and perfected my casting technique that day in an effort to get back in his good graces.

Upon returning home, I was scared to death that he would tell everyone and they would make fun of me but he never mentioned it to anyone. On occasion he would pull his hat down on his head, wink, and I would turn red with embarrassment. Only we two knew what that gesture signified.

# THE ONE THAT GOT AWAY

One time Mrs. Johns allowed us to go behind Danny's house fishing. There was a nice size pond full of fish right behind his house. Usually we could not go fishing by ourselves unless the parental units knew about the water. Mother had not given me permission but I thought since Danny's mother was OK with it, there shouldn't be a problem.

It had recently rained and the bank was slick. We sat there swapping boy tales when all of a sudden my fishing line started singing. Mr. Johns had told us stories of a particular big fish in the pond and I knew I had it hooked. I jumped up and pulled the line tight. Just as I set my feet, I began slipping and tumbled feet first over my head into the pond. All thoughts of my fishing pole disappeared as I surfaced to see Danny reaching out towards me with his pole. I grabbed it while he held onto a sapling and pulled me out of the water. I was sure glad that he was bigger and stronger than me.

Mrs. Johns found some loose clothes and told me to change. I was worried mother would find out that I had went fishing without asking her but to my knowledge Mrs. Johns never mentioned my hooking the big one. To be honest, I think she might have felt guilty for allowing us to go to the pond without being supervised by an adult.

# ADVENTURES ALONG THE AU SABLE RIVER

(The Grand AuSable River)

Our favorite river to fish was the Au Sable River. The water was so lucid that it looked like it was only inches deep but in reality it was well over my head in spots. It was loaded with trout and the water was crystal clear. I loved listening to the water sing as it made its way to Lake Huron. Pine, mighty red oaks, golden oaks, aspens and other trees adorned each side, saluting the water on its journey.

In order to not scare the trout, we always walked quietly, stepping carefully, and wore earth color clothes. We didn't move much and when we talked it was in a whisper. When we had to stir, we attempted to move in slow motion and kept a low profile. Our mission was of the serious nature. We had to provide fish for those starving tourists of the area. Besides, Aunt Mabel paid us a good price for the fresh fish. She had a way of fixing the trout that made your mouth water by just thinking about supper. I often thought if I could discover her secret ingredients, I would start a restaurant.

The brook and rainbow trout would swim with their heads upstream, eating anything that came down through the rapids. It was perfect for our rooster tails, salmon eggs, small red worms, and corn. They were great pan fish and usually were anywhere from ten to eighteen plus inches in length. But don't let their size fool you, they put up a tenacious battle and only surrendered to their fate after a ferocious fight. I liked to catch them because they didn't have scales and were easy to clean, plus they were delicious to eat. The biggest one I ever caught was probably close to twenty inches. Or is that a fishing tale expanded with age?

We always left with our limit and either Danny's mother or Aunt Mabel would fix them. They always paid us the fair price of twenty-five cents each for the fresh food and we usually got to eat our own catch. There is no doubt in my mind that many of the guests at Pine Haven Lodge ate from the bounty of our fishing excursions from that grand ole lady known as the Au Sable.

(AuSable River at Grayling, Michigan)

# THE GREAT TREASURE HUNTER

One of the memories that had been eroded by Father Time was the adventures of the great treasure hunter. I had been down by the AuSable River looking in the sand and rocks for any little shiny object of interest to a young lad. I was not looking for anything in particular but thought something of value might have been washed up on the sand and been trapped by the rocks. I remember my interest peaked in my imaginings but on that day I did not find anything of interest. I was not deterred though. I continued looking whenever I was no longer interested in fishing. As I looked for treasure I would find very smooth flat stones and practiced skipping rocks. I became quite skilled at skipping rocks and was known to have a good arm when it came to contests with the other boys. I was able to skip a rock as many as fifteen to twenty times before the water reclaimed her prize.

I had bent over and reached for a flat rock to skip when I noticed a small round rock half submerged in the sand. I lost interest in the skipping rock and focused my attention on my latest discovery. The stone was perfectly round, smooth and seemed polished. It was the size of a large marble and I decided to put it in my pocket. Upon the appointed time of leaving the area, I jumped on my bike with my trusty Zebco and pedaled towards the house. I loved the feel of the wind blowing in my hair and the way my Schwinn sang to me as we went up and down the hills to our destination.

After I reported in to mother and obtained my rations, I went out to the shop where the men were working. They greeted me with the usual bravado and we talked a few minutes. I told them of my fishing trip and my lack of supplying the family with trout. Then I remembered the stone in my pocket and decided to show it to them. Both men looked at it intently and stated that it looked like an Indian marble. They said that the rock was actually hardened clay and that Indians used them as we did in school.

The newly acquired information thrilled me and I decided to become a treasure hunter. I told my mother of my latest endeavor. I asked mother if she would help me find something to strain the sand whenever I went on one of my outings. I could also use the sifter across the road. I had a large road construction project in progress for my toy cars and trucks. That location was quite sandy and something might have been buried many years ago. She went to the kitchen cabinet and found strainer (colander) with a handle. She said I could have it. I was overjoyed and decided to take my trucks and cars out to play in the sand. While constructing roadways, I planned to sieve for buried treasure. To the best of my recollection, my luck never panned out!

One afternoon Smitty came to me and asked me would I like to go swimming at East Twin Lake. I cannot imagine a youngster refusing such an offer. I asked if I could take my strainer and of course he said yes. We went to the beach and I went splashing into the water. After a few moments I was tired of swimming and decided to treasure hunt. I went along the beach after Smitty instructed me to do a grid search. He explained that I needed to search certain areas so I didn't duplicate my hunt. I marked off a small section with driftwood and started my explorations.

After what seemed to be an eternity, I started feeling discouraged. I guess Smitty saw my disappointment and encouraged me to continue my quest. He helped establish another perimeter and within a few minutes I discovered a nickel. Smitty instructed me to dig in another location and within no time I found a quarter! I was euphoric! I knew that I would never have to work in a shop when all I had to do was hunt buried treasure.

I kept searching and found a few more pennies and a dime before it was time to go. When we arrived home, I ran to the lodge and showed Aunt Mabel my newly acquired treasures. Uncle Pug came from the den to see what all the commotion was about. I showed Uncle Pug my bounty and he seemed quite pleased. Smitty stood in the background with a big smile on his face. I guess he was happy too. Uncle Pug told me if I did all my chores and if my mother would let me go, he would take me to a place where he had found a silver dollar. Well, you didn't have to tell me twice. That week I was a wonder child, doing all my chores and asking mother and Aunt Mabel if there were any other tasks that needed to be completed.

Saturday slowly arrived and true to his word, Uncle Pug knocked on the door and asked if I was ready to go. Heck, I would have taken off in the middle of the night. I was about to enter the inner circle where only men go to find their cache. I was delighted to see that Smitty had decided to go with us. It would be a men's only search. Mother kissed me goodbye (much to my embarrassment) and she went up to help Aunt Mabel at the lodge.

We drove to a lake that I had never seen. Its name eludes me to this day but the beach area was long and beautiful. The men had fishing rods and at the perimeter of the beach, we fished. To be honest, my heart was not into it. I came for treasure. After catching a few blue gills and bullheads, the men decided it was time to let me search the beach area. Again I was instructed on how to sift and how to establish a grid area. I started sifting sand and it seemed everywhere

Uncle Pug instructed me to dig, I would find a coin. He looked over the sandy area, bent down and then summoned me to the spot. Sure enough, I would find a coin. My greatest find was a silver dollar that was dated 1927. I was delighted because the coin was the year of my mother's birth. I needed a present for her and this would be perfect. I found an Indian head nickel and also a one dollar bill that someone must have dropped out of their pocket.

After we exhausted the area, we started home. My total bounty for the day was over four dollars. I always found it strange that whenever I went by myself treasure hunting, I came back empty handed. But on every occasion when I went with Smitty, Uncle Pug, Aunt Mabel or mother, I would find something in the sand. They were my good luck charms and the youthful treasure hunter knew a good thing. Whenever we went out on an adventure by the great lakes, rivers, or lakes within our area, my trusty sifter would be part of my equipment.

I gave my mother the silver dollar and it was one of her favorite gifts. Mother kissed me, Uncle Pug, and then Smitty. I couldn't for the life of me figure out why Smitty and Uncle Pug got a kiss too. Adults are such strange creatures. My treasured coins were placed in the little safe I received on Christmas day.

# ICE FISHING

One of my favorite pastimes during winter was ice fishing. An adult would always go with us and declare if the ice was thick enough to hold our weight. If it was, we were granted fishing privileges after being instructed about respecting the ice and procedures to safeguard against the ice breaking. We were instructed to never go on the ice alone, have a rope tied to an object about fifty feet from you and to listen for loud cracks or booms. We were also told to stay about ten feet apart from one another.

We took our trusty Zebco 33 filled with 8 pound test line. We used minnows, wax worms and corn. We always had a hatchet to cut a hole in the ice (the adults did this for us), needle nose pliers, split shot, bobber stops and lots of snacks. We always walked to the lake area and pulled our supplies out on the ice via our sleighs. We felt like Eskimos going on a winter hunt to supply the village with food. I loved listening to the sound of the well waxed runners of the sled going across the ice. I often wondered what it would have been like to take a running go on the ice with my mighty sleigh. I knew though Mr. Johns, Smitty, or Uncle Pug would not allow such a reckless act.

We dressed quite warmly but found that we couldn't stay out on the lake long due to the cold. If it was really bad, we would take a tarpaulin and build a small windbreaker with it. The adults fished within sight of us and offered hand signals for us to follow. I can't recall how successful we were but I do remember the Northern Pike, Perch, and the occasional Trout caught by the men fishing from the lodge who paid Uncle Pug to show them how to ice fish. The great thing about it was the weather was so cold we didn't have to keep the fish in the water or clean them until we got back to the lodge. I do believe that the greatest joy I had was spending time on the ice with my best friend Frosty, Uncle Pug, Smitty, and the guests. The walk back to the cars was always filled with laughter and talk of the one that got away. On occasion Danny and I would be the subject of a surprise snowball attack from Smitty. As I said before, he had quite an arm on him.

Upon our arrival back at the lodge, Aunt Mabel would have hot chocolate for the boys and coffee for the men waiting. Then she would bring out her special cookies from her magical wood stove. Mother served the men and the conversation was always light. Those were glorious days and the memoires of yesteryear sustains me to this day.

# THE GRAND CANOE RACE

From the first moment I ever saw a canoe, I was hooked. It was all I talked about. I wanted a birch bark canoe like the Native Americans had made but any form of a canoe would meet my requirements. I was at the lodge eating and happened to mention a canoe. I can't remember who said it, but one of the adults at the table asked me had I ever seen a canoe race? I hadn't and the image caught my interest. Smitty said that they have an annual race in Grayling and that if I was good, did all my chores and earned the privilege, he would take us to see it. I was elated. I asked question after question and finally he said he would get some information for me to read but it was my responsibility to study regarding the race.

Smitty kept his word and upon returning from a trip to Grayling, he handed me some material about the race. The race had started in nineteen forty-seven and I thought that so interesting since that was my birth date. It began in Grayling, Michigan, and ended at Oscoda, Michigan, where the great Au Sable flows into Lake Huron. Au Sable! That was my river and my interest was now keen. It was called the Weyerhaeuser Au Sable Canoe Marathon and was considered to be the longest race in the country. It was over one hundred and twenty miles long!

We found out that the race was going to be held in the last week of July and made plans to be there at the starting line to watch the canoes dash into the water. I was very excited and couldn't wait until the race. Finally the day came. I woke up early and got ready to go. To my surprise the event was held in the evening and the participants raced throughout the night. I guess I didn't read the fine print. We spent the entire day in Grayling, Michigan. We shopped around and I saw many people from different areas that were in the race. I wanted to talk to them but was too shy. We went to Hartwick Pines State Park and then ate at a local restaurant.

The race began by the canoe being carried down the streets and then put into the water. The canoers had lights on and soon they disappeared along the river route. We got into the car and followed them, stopping at different points and seeing the lights as they navigated the river. I was fascinated with the sound of the canoes in the water and the sight of the lights on the Au Sable. It was then that I determined when I grew up I would become a famous explorer and canoe down the Amazon looking for lost tribes. I would be another Tarzan to the people and help them fight the bad men trying to destroy their villages.

Our adventure ended between Luzerne and Red Oak where the mighty Au Sable flowed. It was the same location where some of my friends and I used to ride our bikes to fish on so many occasions. Now it had another meaning to me and I couldn't wait until school started back to share my adventure with the guys and of course my teacher, Mrs. Smith.

I watched as the canoes went under the bridge and I bid them farewell for the evening, vowing to join them when I became a man. There was no doubt in my mind that someday I would lead the pack and be victorious in the grand canoe race, as the crowd cheered my success. Even at this stage in life, I still desire to canoe down the Au Sable, but do not relish the thought of the portals. I understand there are six of them now. That is a lot of carrying a canoe for a man of my years!

# SCHOOL DAYS

(Red Oak School-Now a Fire Department)

I attended a one room school in Red Oak, Michigan. It was white and the boards ran horizontally. The classroom was large to me with a big stove as you first entered the room. The hallway had hooks by the wall near the front door where we were to hang our coats. The black board was massive and lived up to its name. The desks were all lined up in a row and the top of the desks folded upwards in the direction of the teacher's desk. Each had their own ink well. There was a back door that we used to go out for my favorite subject, recess!

In 1957, Red Oak School celebrated its fiftieth anniversary. I vaguely recall the details but remember mother, Smitty, Uncle Pug, and Aunt

Mabel driving to Red Oak for an Open House. The reason I remember the escapade was because we students had a field day after we ate while the adults were meeting and eating. This was verified by an email received from Mrs. Hodge (daughter of Mrs. Marie Smith-my teacher) who found the following statement in Mrs. Smith's journal. *"May 25, 1957. I went on up to Open House at Red Oak School – 50 years of school there."* Someday maybe I will be able to discover the total number of students that attended the little one room school nestled on a knoll and the date the doors were closed.

The sanctuary of higher learning is now used by the Red Oak Fire Department. It looks much like it did in the days of my childhood. I wonder what they did with the desks, blackboards, and all the other instructional material stored in that building? I am sure that on occasion the whispers of youthful days are carried on the wind and if you listen with your heart, you can hear the sound of children's play. I know I carried from those walls a sound educational background with a strong motivation to better myself in life.

My first year at Red Oak, there was eight students including myself. Three brothers carried the last name of Kann were also my friends The Cordell family moved in later with six children. They became dear friends of mine.. I didn't know it then but my ancestor was from the Caudill

(Cordell) lineage and I often wonder if we were related and if so, how. Danny Johns and I made up the last of the elite eight. Our teacher was Mrs. Marie Smith. She was a delightful lady who always wore a flower-patterned dress. She was short, full figured, and was determined to teach us with good measure. Now I often ponder was she any relation to Morris A. Smith? I never thought to ask.

(Mrs. Marie Smith)

Her teaching method was excellent. Her philosophy was even better. I recall her stating that if we failed, she failed and that, though we were a small school, we had large hearts. Her round robin reading, spelling bees, math races, home spun games and recess still linger in my mind. She believed in a holistic approach to education. She insisted upon teaching us how to phonetically analyze words and simple rules of English. A couple of her rules I still pass on to my students even to this day. When two vowels

110

go walking the first one does the talking. Another rule was, 'I before e except after c'. She drilled it into our heads the importance of reading and though most of us were average she considered her duty to educate us morally, ethically, academically, physically, and spiritually.

Every Friday she would have the two ladies who lived in the cabin next to the school come over and have Bible class. I believe one of the ladies names was Ms. Shirley. They had an easel with images of different biblical characters and shared stories. We always sung songs of joy. "Jesus loves me this I know for the Bible tells me so," was one. Another song I loved was: "The BIBLE, yes that's the book for me," and of course the classic, "If you are happy and you know it, clap your hands". We would end in prayer and always have a treat after the study. It was wonderful and I must state that never did their teaching infringe upon my rights. In fact I consider freedom to worship AS my right no matter the location. So did the founding fathers of this nation and I will yield to no one in compromising such sacred principles.

Mrs. Smith demanded that we listened to every word and that we showed respect in all things, especially for God, Country, and guest speakers. Her word was considered the gospel to the elite eight. No one dared challenge her and we always kept a keen eye upon her "board of education" that she displayed proudly and prominently above the chalk board.

Mrs. Smith always had a 'duty roster' for her elite eight plus six. Some of the chores were bringing in four buckets of wood/coal daily, serving the food, washing the dishes, sweeping the floor, dusting, pencil sharpening, flag detail, and leading in saying the Pledge of Allegiance. One of the privileged duties was washing Mrs. Smith's car. The temptation to spray your partner was always lurking in the back of our mind, but we were fully aware of the price that would be paid for such an act. I would be so proud when she selected me to assist and take painstaking detail in doing the job to the best of my ability.

We took turns in praying every day before lunch was served. We were allowed to bring our own lunch and most time mother had mine packed in my Lone Ranger lunch bucket. My lunch usually consisted of a peanut butter sandwich, chicken noodle soup (it was always warm in the Lone Ranger thermos), a snack cake, and a drink. On occasion I would have a ham or bologna sandwich. On special occasions I would be given a pop or hot chocolate (Ovaltine) on those cold wintry days. Oh, and then there was Tang! Gosh how I loved that nectar of the Gods and knew by drinking enough of it I too could be an astronaut someday.

There were many occasions in which Mrs. Smith brought us her special homemade soup and it was such a treat. My favorite was her vegetable beef and peanut butter sandwiches. Campbell's couldn't touch her secret recipe! Her extraordinary peanut butter sandwiches were mixed with maple syrup and the flavor was better than a piece of German Chocolate cake. Nothing was better on a cold snowy day than hot soup, sandwich and cold milk to wash it down with. I credit those days for my love of soup and peanut butter sandwiches.

It seemed to me that no matter how deep the snow, we went to school. Danny's dad or mom would drive Danny and me to school. The other six boys lived close and I guess they walked. On occasion, Uncle Pug would get the bobsled out and hook it to the tractor somehow and take us to school. Usually the snow was pretty deep. That was so much fun and I recall pretending to be on a dog sled with the world's largest dog.

To be honest, the snow days were our favorite time of year. It was our creative season. During recess we would go on each side of the road and build forts. Then we would choose sides. Each team ran from the middle of the road to their perspective fort and begin making ammunition (snowballs) as fast as they could. Then the war games began! Snowballs would be launched across the fire lane and if you were hit with one, you were considered wounded, and you were out of the fight. A direct hit in the head meant you had to join the other team. The team with the most people on their side when the bell ended recess was declared the winners. Keeping in mind that there were only eight students in the school, usually the first casualty meant instant a championship for the other team. Still it was great fun. Sometimes Mrs. Smith would come out and join us. We dared never to hit her with a snowball because of the two foot long pine board she displayed to deter such actions. She had a swing with that board of education better than Mickey Mantle or Babe Ruth!

When we weren't fighting at the fort we made snow angels, built snow men, snowball fought, and of course sliding on cardboard boxes. On occasion someone brought an inner tube to school and we would be propelled all the way down the lane. Before we played with the inner tube, it had to be inspected by our teacher. On those special Fridays, after we came in from recess, Mrs. Smith would make snow cream. She always required that we assist her with the ingredients and I considered it a privilege to be the snow gatherer or milk inserter. I still love to make those delicious delicacies to this day. The more I think about it, the more I realize that Mrs. Smith had a sweet tooth too!

Another game we played was called Annie Over. We played this in the fall for some reason. We took up sides and flipped a coin to see who would 'Annie Over' the ball across the roof of the school. Once the ball landed on the other side of the building, the opposing team would charge from both sides. The person with the ball tried to hit a player and have him join his team. Again the team with the most on its side was declared the winner when she rang the bell.

Spring and fall games included King of the Mountain, softball, Red Rover, frozen tag, marbles and a few games we created. I would take my marbles to school hoping to expand my collection. Sometimes I returned with my pockets heavier and some days they would be lighter. In class we played games that Mrs. Smith selected. One was called Tea Kettle. I remember getting so excited about playing it that I made up a little song. I was embarrassed when I noted my teacher looking at me with questioning eyes. We would have spelling bees, and quizzes to see who would move to the head of the class for the week. The topics would be varied and always interesting.

She also believed in doing special art projects. I loved to feel the finger paint between my fingers and palms. I would wipe the various colors on my flannel shirt or blue jeans, much to the dismay and disapproval of mother. I loved working with that wondrous white pasty glue and Popsicle sticks. I would catch her back turned and lick my fingers. I loved that glue but knew better than get caught eating it.

We would also make different seasonal items. We would take clay and learn how to make a bowl. We even created 'Plaster of Paris' objects. Mine always looked lopsided or out of sorts but I was so proud when mother bragged on my unique creations. My greatest creation was a model of a horse but its leg was somehow broken. Still that three legged horse was the talk of the lodge. Now that I think of it, I am sure it didn't look anything like a horse! Funny how much smarter adults get when you find yourself in their shoes.

My all time favorite activity was coloring and her coloring sheets. Mrs. Smith always had coloring sheets and books for us. In our spare time we knew we could get a sheet and color it. On the back of the paper we would have to write a story about the picture but it was worth it just to color.

On one occasion she had us draw and color a map of different countries. I was working very hard on my creation when I felt her presence over my shoulder. Mrs. Smith stated that my map looked great and without thinking I stated that my father had been a map maker in Greece. As soon as I uttered the words I felt embarrassed due to my little white lie. I glimpsed at Mrs. Smith and she had such a look of sympathy on her face, like she knew something I didn't. She stroked my hair and said she was proud of me. I felt terrible and wanted to tell her that I lied but was afraid to do so. I was afraid that she would think less of me and I wanted to be her pet pupil. Even today I wondered why I had to tell such a fib to a lady who gave so much of herself for my growth. Isn't it funny how you can remember the little things in your life?

Another incident that I vividly recall was when it was my time to clean the ink off of the printer. You see, Mrs. Smith believed that the school belonged to us and it was our duty to maintain it. Each week we were given a new assignment and received a grade on how well we completed our tasks. I prided myself in getting those A's and a positive note on my report care.

We had just made our newsletter to our parents and I was to blot off the ink from the roller and the ink on the pan. I blotted the roller but instead of blotting the pan, I rubbed the gel back and forward. To my horror the gel within the container became loose and shredded into pieces. I began sweating bullets. My greatest fear was to face Mrs. Smith and inform her that I had ruined the school's printing press.

Mr. Johns came and for a moment I thought I could just hide the pan and my crime would not be discovered. Then maybe I could blame someone else. I started to the car but my heart refused to follow. I asked Mr. Johns if he would wait just a minute so I could tell Mrs. Smith something. I went in with a burden on my chest that I felt couldn't be removed. Mrs. Smith was working at her desk. I stood there for a moment gathering my thoughts. She looked up above her glasses and asked me had I forgotten anything. I blurted out that I had destroyed her newspaper press and began crying. She smiled at me and simply said that 'accidents happen' and then thanked me for being honest. As I went out the door, the burden was lifted and I felt renewed and forgiven. The more I think of that day, the more I realize that Mrs. Smith taught me another valued lesson of life and that the greatest lessons we learn along the way are about life. I owe her my deepest gratitude and feel her presence whenever I am in the classroom teaching about life.

There is a saying that I feel exemplifies a couple of teachers in my life. One is Mr. Benton Back and the other is Mrs. Marie Smith. The saying goes like this: *"A teacher touches eternity. He/she never knows where his/her influence will end."* Because of Mr. Back and Mrs. Smith, I carry the torch of enlightenment to the rising generation, in hopes that someday they can reflect lovingly on me as I do those who molded my life.

# THE LEGENDARY FRED BEAR

We had many guest speakers at our school. Mrs. Smith believed in community involvement and for her boys to be given the opportunity of knowing about what people did for a living. The speaker I remember the best was Fred Bear, founder of Bear Archery. He was considered to be the greatest bow hunter in the world and had one of the largest collections of archery artifacts in the country. He was awesome and I liked him from the first time I saw him. He looked like such a gentleman in his hat.

He took a special interest in our little school and came out to speak and demonstrate with his bows. He taught us hunting safety and allowed us to shoot at a target. The last day of school before Christmas break, Mr. Bear brought each of us a gift. We were so excited and when we opened the package, we discovered we had the same gift! It was a beginner bow set with a personal note from Mr. Bear. That Christmas I was joy filled. Every night I offered a pray for Mr. Bear's safety and happiness.

My friend and I practiced everyday so we could impress Mr. Bear on his next visit. The other boys who received the Bear bow did so as well.

One of the ways I honed my skills was to get a milk carton, place a rock in the bottom of it, tie a string at the top, and secure it to the old apple tree. I would swing the carton back and forth and step back to release my arrow. As I progressed, I would swing the milk carton and step further back. One time Danny came over and we began practicing. I luckily hit a great shot and he thought I was a terrific archer. I never told him that I couldn't hit the side of a barn at fifty paces. Sometimes we just allow a legend to be born.

Snow did not deter us in our duties to perfect our archery skills. Our work ethics could not be touched by mortal hands. We were determined to win Mr. Bear's favor. I don't think we ever did but he would always smile and say that someday we would have our own museum of stuffed animals. I envisioned winning an archery contest and when I went up against the great Fred Bear, I would purposely lose in honor of his Christmas gift to me and my classmates. That day never came and my skills dwindled as the years crept upon my being.

# NELLIE BELLE

One of my favorite Christmas gifts of all time came from my teacher, Mrs. Smith. For some reason, she decided to give all of us a chicken for Christmas, much to the displeasure of our parents. You see, they were still alive and were loudly protesting being confined under our arms. When Mrs. Johns picked us up from school that evening, she saw the chickens coming in her direction under our arms. Her facial expression immediately demonstrated her displeasure. She stated what on earth she would ever do with a live chicken. Danny just looked at her with a big smile on his face. "Those chickens better not make a mess in this car," she stated with authority. Danny and I looked at each other and tried not to laugh at how mad she would have been if one of our chickens got loose or worse, had an accident.

My beauty was a little red singing hen and I named her Nellie Belle. I named her after Roy Rogers's sidekick's jeep. I think his name was Pat. My little red hen was the cutest thing in my mind but not so in mothers or Uncle Pug. He used to kid me that the hen would do well in a pot of chicken soup rather than in the yard. Aunt Mable would scold him and tell me not to mind his foolishness.

Ole Nellie Belle got to the point she would follow me around begging for handouts and I always obliged her singing with a treat. Frosty was not jealous of my new pet but if given the opportunity, would ruffle her feathers by chasing her around the old workshop or trailer until I put a stop to it. She was a laying hen and mother would gather her eggs from the nest I discovered. She tried to sit one time but mother discouraged her because the eggs weren't fertilized. I wasn't sure what the matter was but I really wanted to have some doodlers running around the yard. Mother did not share the same enthusiasm for that idea though and put her foot down when I mentioned getting a rooster. I told her that I just wanted to hear a rooster crow but I think she knew the real purpose of my request.

I never did know what happened to my Belle. I came home one evening and couldn't find her. I asked everyone and they said they had not seen her that morning. I went all over the area with Frosty hunting for her and calling her name but she never answered my summons. For some reason I got it in my mind that the Swamp Fox must have been involved but I knew Nellie could fly. Surely the Swamp Fox could not do such a feat! I do know that Danny's little hen ended up in a pot for messing around the flower garden at his parent's house! I prefer to think that Nellie Belle went to chicken heaven.

# SMOKEY THE BEAR

Some people state that he doesn't exist. Well, I had the privilege of meeting him and can vouch for him. He is alive and well. 'He prowls and growls and sniffs the air. He can find a fire before it starts to flame. That is why they call him Smokey that is how he got his name.' He came to our class quite unexpectedly. He was none other than the world known celebrity, Smokey the Bear. I recall him vividly. He had his ranger hat on and his trousers, with a shovel. He talked (I was amazed by that!) about fire safety and how we could prevent forest fires. After his lecture, Smokey had us raise our right hands and made us Junior Rangers! I was so excited. Not only had I met a talking bear but I was now an official junior ranger. I had a badge and a card stating I was a guardian of the woods. I just couldn't wait to catch someone being careless with a campfire. I didn't have long to wait.

Uncle Pug and Aunt Mabel had hired me to rake the leaves around the 'island'. The island was a circular drive in front of the lodge. I remember how big it was in my mind and I thought I would never get them raked and moved. I worked hard for those five dollars.

One of the hunting guests was outside smoking and I noted that he threw down a cigarette near some leaves. I went over and as politely as I could be, flashed my badge and told him that the cigarette could cause a fire. He laughed in the strangest manner, said that I was only a boy and shouldn't be telling an adult what to do. I was scared but knew I was right so I went and stamped out the cigarette. He got mad and cursed. Just then Aunt Mabel came to the door and stated firmly that, 'the boy is right' and told me to come to her. I ran over and felt the safety of her hand on my shoulder. The man must have been drinking because he started talking badly to Aunt Mable.

It was then that I caught the image of Uncle Pug coming from around the house. I had heard him talk of his boxing days and knew that he was as strong as an ox. Uncle Pug looked at the man for a second, told him that he did not allow such language around his wife or a child and insisted on the man leaving.

I could tell that the man started to buck but I do believe he saw the demeanor in Uncle Pug's eyes and wisely complied. There was no doubt in my mind that Uncle Pug would have backed up his words with action. That was the only time I saw Uncle Pug that angry and I was the cause of it all. I felt bad about the incident but later was told by Aunt Mabel that standing up for something right is never wrong. I carry that lesson to this day and still protest when I see people discard cigarettes on the ground.

# THE SEARCH FOR LEGENDS

Mrs. Smith, our teacher, was an opportunist. She also had the keenest senses known to mankind. He could detect our whispers at forty yards, which put us on high alert to watch our conversations. She wrote on the board with her back turned and still be able to see any misconduct or off task behavior. I often thought she had a mirror attached to the blackboard but I never could find it.

One day the elite eight were all talking just outside the back door about Indians. Mrs. Smith's desk was close to the exit and I imagine she was all ears. When we went in, she read us a poem about a warrior named Hiawatha. I recognized some of the words because Bugs Bunny used to say them in a cartoon about Hiawatha. Of course Bugs was the star. Elmer Fudd was rabbit hunting in a canoe. Finally Elmer gave up and kissed the rabbit. The following words are still etched in my memory: "By the shores of Gitche Gumee, by the shining Big Sea Water". Mrs. Smith said the poem was written by a man called Longfellow. I was hooked. It was then that I vowed to become a famous poet when I grew up and share my talent of poetry with the world. My first poem went like this: "It's no disgrace to be ugly in the face; you're part of the human race, so run!" Needless to say, I am still perfecting my poetry abilities!

After reading she gave us an assignment of looking up in our books, stories about Native American Indians. We did what we could with limited resources and then she gave us a project. We were to interview local people of our county and ask them about Indian stories they might have heard. We were to report back on Monday. This was not an option and no excuses would be accepted for not doing what she expected.

I went to the lodge and began asking Uncle Pug and Smitty about any legends or did they know where a burial ground was located. Uncle Pug stated that he didn't know of any burial grounds in the county but he was sure they fished the mighty Au Sable and with all the game, the area would have been a great hunting ground. That made sense but I wanted a story. I asked Smitty and soon I realized that he had started spinning a yarn and I knew I could not use it. He was always 'pulling my leg' in some manner.

I was beginning to doubt if I could find any useful information until I mentioned my search at the little store in Red Oak. One of the old timers was sitting around and overheard me. He asked me had I ever been to the burial grounds in the area. I didn't know what they were so he told me that the Indians of the area would bury their dead as soon as possible so that the warrior could make his trip to the afterlife. The journey took four days and started once the warrior was buried. I asked him how women and children were buried and he shrugged his shoulders saying only that warriors hunted the area and as far as he knew, there was not a camp in the county during those days of old.

I started wondering if maybe the place where the tribe lived had not been discovered and what if they were hidden deep within the forest. This sparked my imagination and before long I began looking for the lost tribe. I wasn't sure what tribe they were but I knew they were out there. My search took me ever deeper into the black pine forest.

On Monday we went in to offer our reports and everyone had a great Indian legend. I began sweating bullet shaped beads because my information was not a legend but more factual in nature. I remember when it was my turn; I began talking nervously about what I had found. I told what Uncle Pug and Smitty had said but I didn't relate the wild tale Smitty tried to sell me. Even I wasn't that gullible. I talked about the old man at the country store and what he said, and then I sat down knowing I would get a big E on my report.

After all the reports were given, Mrs. Smith called each of our names and commented upon our stories, legends, and information. She corrected some of the mistakes and discussed the difference between fact, fiction, and legend. She then offered our grade to us orally.

When it was my turn to be analyzed, I was a nervous wreck. I did not like to fail and I knew my report was not what she wanted. She began by explaining that she was unaware of any tribes having an established living quarters in the county. She stated that the Native American Indians that I described were of the Ojibway, or more commonly known in our state as the Chippewa tribe. I had never heard of either. She declared that as far as she knew my information was right about that particular tribe but different tribes had different rituals, practices and we must never be inclusive with our thoughts about people. She told us that the Chippewa lived around the St. Ignace and Sault Saint Marie Area. There was a reservation for the Ottawa at Little Traverse Bay. There were Fox Indians in Michigan but the Native American Indian of our area was known as the Potawatomi.

My heart sank. I knew I had the wrong tribe and that more than likely I would fail. Mrs. Smith wrote in her grade book and then looked at me. She smiled and said she was proud of my details and did I like Native history. I beamed and said I loved it. She said she could tell. She said that because of my effort and information I would get an A on the project. I was so comforted. After our reports had been completed Mrs. Smith pulled out another book from her book bag and read a story to us about the ways of the people known as Native Americans.

After sharing the story, she challenged us to continue learning and reading about other people so we would have a better understanding. I had no problem with that and vowed to find that lost tribe, now known to me as the Potawatomi, in my area.

Each time I went to the woods I searched for the people of the lost tribe. I even went to different areas and on occasion could hear the chants of the children playing along the Au Sable River or the drums of medicine men performing a sacred ritual. I found myself wishing I could be Native like Iron Eyes Cody or Jay Silverheels. Maybe I had such bloodlines coursing in my veins and someday I would discover my heritage.

I have loved their heritage ever since that date. I can honestly say that the six years I spent on the Navajo and other reservations were forged in a little one room school house in Red Oak. My search for my pedigree was a direct result of those elementary days when we were challenged by a visionary teacher known simply to this fielder as Mrs. Marie Smith.

# SCHOOL FIELD TRIPS

Mrs. Smith always arranged field trips that were more like family outings. They always had an educational value to them and we prepared for the trip by learning about whatever the topic of discussion was. A well-versed mind is a well-trained one, she would mutter. She would get the parents who drove (mother would always ride with Mrs. Johns, Danny and I) and have them take us to different places. I remember getting so excited when she told us that we could earn a trip to the Shetland pony farm if we all did well the next two weeks. I took every book home and doubled my study time. I didn't even watch T.V. for that week. Mother thought I must be coming down with something.

We all met Mrs. Smith's objectives and the day of the field trip finally arrived with much fan fare. Smitty sneaked and gave me some money. He didn't know it but Aunt Mable did the same thing. I felt rich, with almost ten dollars in my pocket.

We were told to wear our cowboy hats and boots. I even strapped on my trusty Lone Ranger silver handled revolvers and put my mask in my pocket just in case some banditos came by while we were on our trip. They would not have stood a chance with the gang of eight Rangers that day. We all met at school and off we went. The Kahn boys were with their parents, the Cordell boys with theirs and I with the Johns.

It seemed like it took forever to get there but it was worth the ride. The farm was covered with fences and the first little pony I saw stole my heart. His long tight mane was a light tan and flowed almost to his knees. His tail barely missed the ground and was the same color as his mane. He was a golden shade and I just knew his name had to be Trigger. I was right. When the man came to welcome us he called 'Little Trigger' and he came running. Shetlands have a reputation of being highly intelligent. Trigger certainly was. To our delight, Trigger performed a couple of tricks. He counted for us! He got on a stand with his two front hooves and offered up the cutest whiney. I wanted that pony so badly.

The owner took us to the barn and told us about the different types of ponies he had. He was very knowledgeable and to this day I can tell you about some of them. During his presentation, the man stated that the ponies originated in Isles off of Scotland. He said that they ranged anywhere from twenty-eight to forty-two inches high. He informed us that horses are measured in hands and that forty-two inches would be about ten hands high. I remember going home and measuring everything in hands. He said they come in every color and some pull small buggies. They are very strong for their size. He had a buggy ready and he had someone take a couple of us at a time for a ride. It was wonderful.

Then he took us to a small corral. There he had four ponies with saddles on their backs. I got so excited. He told about how you have to take care of the horse and how to 'gear up' the saddle. He showed us how to mount and then he had us line up and we were allowed to ride.

I picked the one that looked like Silver and I began the journey of capturing Butch who had killed my brother. I envisioned Silver standing on his hind legs, as Tonto followed closely behind in hot pursuit of those soon to be banished outlaws. I wanted to ride forever but in a few moments, reality returned as it was someone else's turn. But my imaginings continued for months from the experience of that day. Every time we went towards the farm area, I asked Smitty or Uncle Pug could we drive by and see the 'baby horses' out in the field. I think they liked to see them too. Maybe they wanted to ride them and pretend to be Gene Autry the singing cowboy.

Time slipped by very quickly and before we knew it, Mrs. Smith said it was time to leave. After saying goodbye to our mounts and thanking the nice people of the ranch, we reluctantly got back into our vehicles.

We drove a few miles and stopped at a restaurant for lunch. The restaurant had a small gift shop and I saw a plastic pony that I wanted. It was black and about the size of Silver (the Lone Ranger's Horse) I had at home. I had the money but still had to beg mother in order to buy it.

The power of peer pressure won out and I went running to the gift shop. Mrs. Smith's look made me return to my seat and I walked back. She didn't say anything but I knew what she was thinking. Rules are to be followed in and out of the class. She nodded in approval. There was only one black plastic horse left and I went up to pay for my newest mount with the pride of purchasing a thoroughbred. Each of us was thrilled with our purchase.

Finally, I left the restaurant full of food and possessing a new trophy that would be corralled with my herd. On rainy evenings or snowy days when I was alone with my imagination, I would saddle up each mount in turn and ride the winds, while chasing those vicious villains away from our little log cabin. All this and more was done by a child of promise while safely snuggled beneath the shadows of the whispering pines.

# A STAR IS BORN

I remember another time when we went to be on a T.V. show. I had never been inside a television studio before and was scared to death. My jaw was quivering. The good news was that the other boys were nervous too. Mr. Roberts (I believe his first name was Kenny but don't believe it was the country singer) was the Master of Ceremonies and he was a singing "jumping" cowboy. Besides Fred Bear and Smokey, he was the most famous person I had ever met. I was so tense that he might ask me to do a duet with him because the boys said I could sing and they may have told him. To my relief he did not. He opened up his show with a song. I still remember the melody and words.

*"Oh I'm going down the country, gonna' a have a lot of fun. Got a penny in my pocket just to buy some chewing gum".*

He interviewed us individually and I recall how frightened I was of that big camera looking at me but before long Mr. Rogers made me feel right at home. He said he liked my flannel shirt and cowboy hat (Lone Ranger special). I remember saying I liked his too. He asked me would I trade and I said no. Everyone laughed. I didn't though, for I was being serious.

# MAPLE TREE FARM

One day after lunch, we had a special treat. Mrs. Smith brought a jar of maple syrup for our dessert. I believe it was one of the Cordell boys asked Mrs. Smith where maple syrup came from. She said that instead of teaching us about it she would show us. In a few days she came in with the announcement that we were going on a field trip to a maple tree farm. I was shocked to hear that trees produced syrup but didn't voice my ignorance. Again we studied about different trees and things you could make from them. I learned about aspirin and which tree bark you could chew on to ease a head ache. God must have made a pharmacy with all those healing trees and plants.

The day finally arrived when once again we climbed into our parents vehicles and rode a few miles to a lovely farm. I noted that the trees were all lined up in rows and that each tree had a shaft coming from it. The man and woman came out of a large house and greeted us. They welcomed us to their farm and began explaining the long process of making maple syrup. I noticed they were dressed in different clothes and the man had a beard. The woman wore a dress and had her hair put up in a bun. The farm was located somewhere around the Mio or McKinley, Michigan, area I believe.

The first step in making maple syrup is in selecting the right size tree. It has to be around eight inches in diameter to sustain a tap. A hole is drilled into the side of the tree for the syrup to drip into a bucket. Then he said you had to boil it. It seemed to me to be a very long process but once we got to taste the pure maple syrup on pancakes, I was sold.

One of my class members asked if it hurt or killed the trees and the farmer explained that the process did not. I had a smarty mouth (my mother's terminology) moment and thought how he would know, he wasn't a tree, but I knew not to voice such a statement in front of Mrs. Smith. It would have been my undoing. He stated that the season for sap running was only four to five months. Again this is a child's recollection. Before we left, he and his wife gave a small bottle of maple syrup to take home for our pancakes. I admit I sampled it unbeknownst to the driver. Danny didn't tell because he sampled his too.

Going home I started thinking that I could grow my own trees and have all the pancakes and syrup I wanted plus make money by selling what I didn't eat. I was sure that the lumberjacks would frequent my establishment and taste the wonderful maple syrup and my special recipe pancakes made to perfection.

# FERRY ACROSS THE MAC

One of the field trips that Mrs. Smith took us on was to a magical place where two of the Great Lakes converge. At the northern tip of Michigan, Lake Michigan and Huron are entwined. Mrs. Smith had us study about the bridge that was being built across the straits and she informed us if we read over one hundred books we were eligible to go. That was no problem for this old boy and I didn't allow my poor reading skills interfere with passing the questions asked by Mrs. Smith about the books. Mother, Aunt Mabel, and Smitty read to me and verified that I knew the stories. I read to them and answered questions about the books. It was a glorious time of anticipation.

Finally the day arrived with the whole school went on a massive pilgrimage to the straits. The trip was approximately one hundred miles but it seemed longer. Upon arriving, I was aghast as to the size of the lakes. I had never seen such a large body of water. I knew there weren't any sharks because we had been taught the water was fresh but there was no doubt in my mind something lurked within the depths that would love to eat a young morsel for dinner. I didn't get to close to the edge of the ferry because the waves were so big. I thought I was getting sea sick but it probably was my imagination.

We were allowed to go into a shop or two but I didn't have much money. I remember one of my friends buying me a small snow bowl with St. Ignace, Michigan, inscribed. I thought it was a pure treasure. Wish I could remember who gave me the money so I could thank them for the gift.

On our way home we talked of the grand adventure and how big the bridge was going to be when finished. I couldn't wait to cross it. I called it the world's biggest swinging bridge and everybody laughed. Mrs. Smith explained that in eastern Kentucky there were swinging bridges to cross the creeks and that was what I was talking about. She saved me from being embarrassed.

When we got home I couldn't wait to show Aunt Mabel my prize and tell her all about the trip. To my surprise everyone in the family sat down on the couch while I sat on the talking pool seat telling of our adventures. I felt I was the king of the castle and when I showed them my treasure, I never heard so many 'oohs and aaws' in all my life. I decided right then and there that I would learn how to construct a bridge bigger than the one being built at the straits and would become famous for my endeavors.

# SILVER DOLLAR PANCAKES

I loved pancakes or flap jacks, as Uncle Pug called them. He started me off in eating them. Aunt Mabel made what she called silver dollar pancakes. They were about the size of a silver dollar and we men would have a contest to see who could eat the most. I received quite a bit of notoriety at the lodge in my ability to put them away.

Once Danny came by to play and we started talking about the delicacies. I bragged on my prowess of eating and he challenged me to an 'eat off'. Now he was larger than me and I had previously seen his ability to wolf down food but I believed I could take him. We asked Aunt Mabel if she would fix them and she agreed. Smitty came in and upon hearing the challenge, stated he would be honored to judge the contest.

Well the battle of the bulge began with a flurry of ingestion of those silver dollar delights. I must admit that Danny was quite nimble with his eating prowess but I had a secret manner in which I ate them. Danny threw in the towel on silver dollar number twenty-three. I ate a couple more just to rub it in that I was the champion. The secret of my pancake eating ability remains with me today though I am officially retired from competition. I will offer a hint to the reader though. It is not in the manner in which you swallow them, it is the technique in chewing without getting choked. The key is the syrup. Utilizing pure one hundred percent maple syrup is imperative.

At school Danny and I shared our competition with our buddies and Mrs. Smith overheard us. She said that she would have a school wide event the following Friday and even get a trophy for the winner. I knew that award would be mine. Like a true Olympian, I began my work out. I practiced every morning for a week on eating only flapjacks. I limited my intake of syrup and butter. My love for pancakes diminished but my desire to win the cup was enhanced by the smell of pending victory.

The imposing day of the Great Silver Dollar Flap Jack Contest came. To my surprise, Mrs. Smith had invited adults from the community to witness the event. My stomach churned with excitement and my eyes was glued on the trophy. Mrs. Smith had employed a couple of volunteers to assist in making the pancakes. She lined up our chairs in one big row and on a given signal we were off to the races. The goal was to see who could eat the most in five minutes. The other boys were amateurs in comparison to my method. I left them behind by five pancakes. I was heading for an easy victory when I felt my stomach rumble. There was an uneasiness and queasiness that I had never experienced while eating pancakes. I continued eating trying to ignore the imminent warning signs. Surely I would be able to show those mere mortals how superior I was in engulfing the meal of my favorite morsels.

I continued cramming them in my mouth and when I looked up at the clock we only had about thirty seconds to go. Then it hit with full force. I felt my body attempting to purge itself even with my pleading protests. Give me thirty more seconds, I demanded of my digestive system, but it was not to be. I found myself not only vomiting with the force of jet propulsion but I also managed to clear the area's population. I was humbled by the involuntary action of my stomach and went home with my first and only loss in the silver dollar pancake eating contest. Since that moment my taste for pancakes has declined and I am retired (self imposed!) from any competition of that or any nature involving gorging myself. Lesson learned.

# TREATS AND TRICKS

One of the special treats our teacher would give us was to walk with us to the little Red Oak store and get some candy. If you didn't have any money, Mrs. Smith would have you work to earn it. *'A penny earned is worth more than a penny borrowed'* was one of her favorite statements. Sometimes she would buy all of us a soda and I thought she must be rich. My favorite was the grape. I also loved those chewable wax coke bottles with the different flavors inside. I would always get Bazooka gum and a candy bar with the understanding that the paper went in the trash and gum is to be disposed of in the proper manner. She was a stickler for rules and would enforce them swiftly no matter who was with us.

Mrs. Smith ran a tight ship. She believed that if she spared the rod she would spoil the child. She also believed in communication with parents on a daily basis. I will never forget the first time I caught her wrath. I am not sure exactly what I did wrong but I do recall the adjective I used, which immediately caught her attention. Her ears went to point like a German Shepherds and she immediately dropped what she was doing to tend to the task of disciplining one of her lambs.

She decisively scolded me and flashed her famous 'board of education', which she could swing with precision. She offered me no quarter and raised the black flag. Three licks later I was in shock as to her strength in wheeling the infamous board.

Even though we didn't have a phone, when I arrived home mother met me at the door with the dreaded question of what went on at school. This was not a dinner table topic but one of inquisition. There was no room for compromise or exaggerations. The truth would be the only thing that could set me free. I did the only thing that I consider prudent and immediately blurted out the word I had recently acquired. You could have knocked her over with a feather. For a moment she simply glared at me in shock and dismay. Then came the raging tongue lashing!

I shall never forget my mother's speech regarding how it hurt her so to think her son would shame our good name. She used to tell me when I left in the mornings for school that she couldn't give me anything other than a good name and she expected to receive it back as good or better upon my return. Like most children do, sometimes in their lives, I must have disappointed that good woman on several occasions. I could see in her eyes at that moment I was not her favorite person and would have to figure out how to get back into her good graces.

I remember mother taking me to the dreaded apple tree and cutting a switch. Usually I had the honor of selecting my branch of punishment and I had become fairly good in distinguishing those less painful. This day however she took the responsibility upon her shoulders. I can still taste the sting of the twig on my legs as we walked back to the cabin but most importantly mother crying. Each step ended with a swipe and mother sobbing. I was a tad confused though when she stated that it hurt her worse than it did me. I kept looking up the hill to see if Aunt Mabel was watching and maybe come to my rescue. She was not and she did not. I was alone with my bruised ego and smarting legs. I was the one nursing the marks on my legs and behind, along with my pride. Mother took me inside for another round of her one sided conversation.

Suddenly she simply pointed in the direction of the bedroom and told me to go to bed. I went licking my wounds, with my tail tucked between my legs. I found the night restless and my worry about my broken hearted mother was too painful for me to contemplate. I wondered if mother would tell Aunt Mabel or Uncle Pug of my sin. Mother must not have because it was never brought up again. All I know is, from that moment forward, certain "flowery" words do not cross my lips.

# BATMAN'S HALLOWEEN

Most youngsters have fond reflections about Halloween. I am no exception. I enjoyed the candy and other treats but my favorite part of the season was getting prepared for the event. Also, I took great pleasure in the car ride back and forth to the houses of the area. Sometimes we would go to Lewiston and walk the streets or Mio and go door to door. Those were the days.

Mother and Aunt Mable would always create a new costume for me. One year I was a cowboy of course but most of the time my costumes were custom made. I guess my favorite was the Batman outfit that mother made. She worked so hard on the ears and eyes slits being just right. When she finished, we went up to the lodge and Aunt Mable made a witches' brew of dye to match the color of the cape. She had embroidered the Batman logo and after the dye had set, mother and Auntie took on the task of hemming and sewing on the 'official' batman insignia. I couldn't wait to try it on! Once I donned the dark knight's suit, I became empowered to do all types of acrobatics, much to the delight of the ladies.

I don't think Uncle Pug was too thrilled though. He just sat on the couch as he read his paper and grunted in acknowledgement of my super human feats. His grumblings did not deter my excitement from building. Finally I was allowed to go outside, much to the relief of my uncle, and explore the Gotham City lurking within my mind.

I didn't need Halloween to become the hero of the night. For three weeks, I hit the ground running to the house from school and immediately begged mother for permission to put on my outfit and fight crime in the yard. I honestly think she got a big kick out of my contortions and gyrates outside, because I would watch her watch me fight with the Joker or Penguin while she sat at the table drinking coffee. Frosty would have to take on those villainous roles, as I chased him around the yard to his delight. He would bark and dare me to catch him by running to my feet and then running off. He was elusive but he did not understand the great mind that he was combating. I would eventually catch him and wrestle him to the ground where he would offer his surrender by licking my face. Anyway to win the battle was my motto.

My first Halloween trip to Mio, Michigan, was exciting. I was dressed in my full regalia and was ready to go with my family. I believe Danny had been grounded and the others were not allowed to go that far from home. I remember Smitty having paint on his face and he looked like a cat. He was silly looking I thought. Mother had a witches outfit on and aunt Mable was dressed like a queen. Uncle Pug chose to go as himself and I knew everyone would recognize that disguise. We parked our car near the Mio Shrine and mother kept reminding me to slow down. I was bouncing all over the place and couldn't wait to knock on my first door.

We went along the local businesses and my bag was getting full. Folks always laughed at Smitty and told mother and Auntie how lovely they looked. I didn't have to tell them though; they knew that they were the most beautiful queen and witch around. One house in particular was decorated with grand fanfare. It possessed spider webs on the porch; hay with three goblins all around the banisters and next to the door was a hideous creature sitting in a rocking chair. The lights were off except for the one shining through the glass on the door. Smitty told me to go on the porch to knock. I was leery but the lure of candy was just too strong.

I went up and knocked and this little old lady with a hump on her back came out with a bag of candy. She talked in a shrill voice and had ghoulish makeup on her face. I was ready to leap out of my skin but she did have some of my favorite candy in her candy dish. She reached out her dish in my direction and told me to help myself. The temptation was too much for the 'sugar-holic' within my body. I reached out and to my dismay; the ghoulish creature who sat in the rocking chair suddenly moved. Oh Lord it was alive! The sinister thing grabbed my hand before I could react and all I could do was let out the cry of a banshee. I don't know how I mustered the strength but I got away from that thing while screaming loudly as I ran.

Smitty was bent over double laughing and I could hear the other adults bursting their sides with laughter. I didn't see a thing that was funny and tried to protest to Uncle Pug who was gasping for air from my fright.

They all got into the car and I took what mother used to call the "bad case of the pouts" to the point that mother asked Uncle Pug to pull over to the side of the road. I knew what was coming, as she took me for a little walk. When I returned to the vehicle I was in a much better mood though it had been forced upon me. That night I learned that adults have a great sense of humor and sometimes their jokes are at the expense of kids. Also know your limits. Lessons learned.

## ON BEING ILL WHEN WELL

I can still taste the cure-all medicine that my mother insisted upon me taking when sick. To beat it all, so did my Auntie. It was disgusting. I remember my first dose and indeed whenever it was mentioned, I was feeling much better regardless. It was called Castor Oil and unfortunately was administered freely upon the first symptom of illness.

My first dose came when I really didn't want to attend school due to a test. I was not a good reader and in fact was scared of reading out loud. We were to read to some community leaders that day and I really didn't wish to show my weakness in that area. So I faked an illness. I knew that Danny got away with faking sickness and his plan seemed sound. His acting abilities and power of persuasion was quite convincing. Some of the symptoms he taught me included the hacking cough, hinting of having the dreaded diarrhea, running nose, fever induced by a hot wash cloth, pitiful weak voice and on occasion having your hands tremble. His plan was fool proof and sound. I believed that I could perform with the best of actors and my time had come to demonstrate my newly acquired skills. I guess my skills were too effective though.

My complaints and pseudo-symptoms led my mother to believe that I needed the concoction.

This was my first taste of the remedy and I thought sure it would kill me. Mother held my nose and rubbed my throat so I would swallow it. I fought gallantly but to no avail. I gagged but somehow kept the brew from being sprayed twenty feet across the floor.

Her next feat was to get Vicks Vapor Rub and apply it all over my body. I felt like a chicken getting buttered for the oven. She then heated up a pan of water, boiled the salve in it and put it on the floor. She instructed me to place a towel over my head, sit in the chair and inhale. To add injury to insult, she put Vicks under my nose and the vapor sensation cleared my lungs of all debris. The final offense was when she gave me a finger full of the salve and instructed me to eat it. The slim seemed to meander down my throat while my body protested. All I can remember of that is the roar of my stomach in protest.

Mother went to the pantry and got out the world famous miracle food for me to eat. I must admit I love Campbell's Chicken Noodle Soup. She fixed a steaming bowl and I devoured it thinking it would get rid of the taste in my mouth. To my shock, it only heightened the rumblings in my tummy and the three different medicines began to compete with each other for supremacy. I imagined that they were three gun slingers fighting for control of the 'stomach town'. My prayers were on the soup but I feared the evil guns of the Castor Oil or

Vicks would prevail. The fighting intensified as the rumblings of my stomach gave testimony, and I knew I could not contain order any longer. With a sudden surge I expelled all three gunfighters from 'stomach town' and lay exhausted upon the floor. For some reason mother was smiling. Then she said something strange. *'What don't kill you will only make you stronger'.* I wasn't sure of what she meant but I decided I was well enough to go to school.

As Uncle Pug, Aunt Mabel, and mother accompanied me, mother told the story of my miracle cure and I was so puzzled at the snickering and Uncle Pug's comment of, *'I told you it would work'.* I entered the school building in time to share my limited talents and with a renewed conviction that I would not miss school ever again. Lesson learned.

# SUMMER WITH THE SMITHS

I must have been eight or nine that summer. Mother had to return to Kentucky due to the death of someone in the family. I did not want to go and protested. Aunt Mabel stated that I was welcome to stay with them at the lodge while mother went to visit her brothers and sisters. Mother thought about it and finally decided that she need not take me to witness such a sad occasion. I was allowed to stay and once again I got my special room at the top of the stairs facing west. I went with Smitty as he took her to the Greyhound Bus Terminal. Mother continued to remind me about being good, washing behind my ears, and always wearing clean underwear in case I had an accident and had to go to the hospital. I never did understand why. Her last instruction was the most pointed. She said I better listen to every word that Uncle Pug and Aunt Mabel said or the wrath of the Lord would be upon my head when she returned. I assured her that I would be on my best behavior. We talked about her return and she promised me that we would go visit the Straits of Mackinac again before school started.

We arrived at the bus terminal and had to wait. The smell of diesel fuel permeated the terminal and for some reason I thought it smelled good. Smitty checked her luggage and then we waited until the announcement came of the bus departing for Detroit. I was a little scared; as this was the first time I was away from my mother. She reassured me with a kiss and hug. Smitty's hand on my shoulder eased my uncertainty. With one final warning regarding my behavior, she climbed aboard the Greyhound and found a seat next to the window. She waved and smiled as the bus left the loading ramp. We had a tearful goodbye but I was confident that she would be back in a couple of weeks.

Smitty took me to get an ice cream and for some reason I remember getting a double dip of chocolate on a sugar cone. We stopped by Smith's bridge on our way home and looked for fish swimming in the current. There was an older couple wading in the water with a dog chasing sticks thrown by his master. So much for seeing fish, I thought to myself.

Upon my return to the lodge, my nostrils detected the smell of chocolate cake and when I rushed into the kitchen; my eyes confirmed that I was in for a treat. Aunt Mabel had my special area cleared and a piece of cake ready for me. She went to the freezer in the back and brought out ice cream. With a wink and a pat on the head I was told to dig in and enjoy. I followed her directive to the letter. With what Smitty had bought me, I believe that was the most ice cream I had ever consumed in one setting. The truth is that I could do that every day without blinking! Based on the first day, I surmised that it was going to be a great summer filled with fun and adventure.

My kingdom expanded during the time of my mother's absence. Aunt Mabel was the best playmate and played marbles with me. She even taught me how to play checkers. Smitty helped me build a birdhouse and Uncle Pug taught me how to whittle. He let me borrow a knife and tutored me regarding the proper protocol of whittling and handling a knife. We would sit in front of the workshop and whittle a piece of cedar or pine in the evenings. He always made something pretty but my product was an effort in futility. We all played board games like Chinese checkers and I learned how to fly a kite. Smitty continued to make his world famous spaghetti and meatballs for us on Wednesday. I bet I gained ten pounds that summer!

Danny would come over and we would go out to the glen but it seemed that we were always being 'eyeballed' by some adult from the lodge. One evening we were treated to an ice cream in Mio and then were allowed to go fishing. Even Uncle Pug joined in on the trip with Smitty. It turned out to be the boy's evening out. I caught a large pan fish that Uncle Pug called a sunfish. It was a big one and barbed me with its fin. I was so proud of that fish. I was able to catch two more keepers. Danny caught his usual limit of trout and we took them home for Aunt Mable to fix. Uncle Pug cleaned them and I must admit we had a grand fish fry. For some reason, fish always tasted better when they were fresh from a babbling brook or rapid running river.

Uncle Pug had a twenty-two rifle that his father owned. He was very proud of that old rifle. It was a Stevens and was made in nineteen-twelve. One afternoon we were doing something around the old saw mill. He looked at me and asked if I had ever shot a gun before. I informed him I had not. He told me to follow him up to the lodge and wait in the circle. The circle was a grass island surrounded by the dirt road. Whenever I played there, I often imagined myself on a deserted island surrounded by an ocean filled with sharks. My only hope of crossing over was to build a raft. An old piece of wood served as my vessel to freedom.

Soon Uncle Pug came out with that old gun and we walked in the direction of the fort. He told me about gun safety and then showed me how to hold the rifle. He put up a target and after demonstrating how to shoot, he looked at me, and said it was my turn. I was a nervous wreck. I thought sure it would knock me down when I pulled the trigger but all it did was made my ears ring a little. He let me shoot the gun a few more times and each time instructed me on how to improve my aim. I was hooked. I was determined to have a gun like that someday.

When mother came home my first request was for a twenty-two or at least a BB gun. It was denied on the grounds that I was too young to be shooting a gun. If she only knew that locked inside of that young body was a fledgling gun fighter. How could the Lone Ranger's number one fan fight outlaws without a weapon? Her wisdom prevailed and I had to wait a couple of years before receiving my first BB gun.

The other thing I remember is a picnic we had by what I thought was the ocean. The water was so clear, the waves so white, and I couldn't see the land on the other side. In actuality we went to Lake Huron. I believe it was in the Black River or in the Alcona area but I am not one hundred percent positive. All I knew was that it was the most beautiful sandy beach and the wind gently kissed my skin. The gulls and ducks dived for their lunch in a lake filled with God's bounty.

We ate out of the picnic basket that Aunt Mabel had fixed. She was the best cook in the world and prepared enough food for a small army. After we ate, we had to wait before going into the water. Auntie said that I would have to wait for one hour. That was a long time for a boy wanting to burst the waves open! After the longest hour of my young life, I was allowed to swim. I waded out a long ways from shore and the water was only up to my shoulders. I was cautioned not to go any deeper. Smitty swam around me like a dolphin guarding its young from a shark attack. On occasion, he would dive, grab my leg, much to my fright and delight. Aunt Mabel wouldn't get in the water but Uncle Pug did. I was amazed at how strong he looked and how well he was able to get around in the water. For an old man he was in great shape and there was no doubt he could whip Dempsey or Sugar Ray.

The evening sun touched the horizon signaling that it was time to go. I sat in the back seat with Aunt Mabel and we rolled down the window. The wind sang a lullaby that made me want to lay my head in Aunt Mabel's lap. I did so and before I was aware of anything, I was sound asleep. The joy of the day ended by my being carried upstairs and tucked into bed by Smitty.

Every day was an adventure filled with amazing discoveries. I learned about the different ferns which grew all around the lodge and our cabin. I was taught how to recognize different animal sounds, calls, tracks and bird songs. I was advised on finding shelter when a thunder storm rolled in but never be under a tree during lightning. I watched Aunt Mabel cook and helped by bringing her eggs and items from the storage area. On occasion, I was allowed to lick the bowl when she made peanut butter candy.

Before long I started missing my mother and wondered when she would return. It was usually when it was bed time. When I asked, someone would say it would be very soon. I loved all the undivided attention I was getting, yet I missed hearing mother's voice read to me or sing to me. There is something about a mother's love and touch that transcends all other boundaries.

One morning after breakfast, Smitty said for me to go with him and that he had a surprise. I went for a ride and we drove towards Grayling. When I saw the sign Greyhound Bus Terminal, I knew what my surprise was going to be. I was not disappointed, as my mother stepped off the bus and came into the terminal. I ran to my mother's arms. Her smile welcomed me along with a hugn and kiss. As usual she had bought me a little trinket to commensurate her trip and her love for her 'Snookems'. Though I loved my time with the Smith's, I missed the times alone my mother that I shared and once again embraced life in the cabin under the shade of the whispering pines. I had it made in both worlds.

# MY FIRST CHRISTMAS IN THE PINES

I had never seen a winter in the wilderness before. The snow came early and lingered on the ground. That did not detour or dismiss school. We went every day. If Mr. Johns couldn't take us in his station wagon, Uncle Pug, or Smitty would get the tractor and pull the old toboggan through the snow and on occasion, the drifts. At school we drew names for a Christmas gift and I got one of the Kahn boys. Mrs. Smith, my teacher, set a limit on our purchase of five dollars. I went to Grayling, Michigan, with mom and Smitty to shop for the present. I found a great bat and ball within my budget and decided it would be a grand gift. It cost a little more than the limit set by Mrs. Smith but I felt the gift was worth it. I was correct in my assumption. He loved it and his parents came over and thanked me personally. I felt so good about giving something that I really wanted to a friend. I think that is the true spirit of Christmas.

Mrs. Smith believed in singing Christmas carols and she listened to the old radio she brought from home. It had tubes in it and the station would drift in and out but it brought a festive mood to the classroom. Sometimes she would burst out in song and demand that we sang along with her. One time she even arranged for a hayride and we went singing Christmas carols to the small community around Red Oak, Michigan. Imagine eight boys, some going through pubescence, singing carols along the highway and to anyone who would stop and listen. I am sure we sang off key and the crooning was staggering at times but the gesture was grand. To me, it was a delightful experience and I used that memory of a time long ago when I taught. We would plan, practice, and participate in annual hay rides behind a wagon pulled by the school principal at Campbell's Branch Elementary.

Mrs. Smith also allowed us to decorate the rooms while we listened to the tube radio, and her singing. We joined in unison with her vocalizations. I do recall her having a lovely high pitched voice and she could hold a note forever. We cut out stars, strung popcorn, gathered up holly branches with bright red berries and painted pine cones for the tree. She would have a tree brought to the school by her husband and we would get a bucket, fill it with rocks, and water once we had the tree perfectly straight, stack the rocks around the tree to hold it in place. We were then instructed on how to water the tree and fire safety. Everything had a lesson for life is what Mrs. Smith would always state. With the lighting of the tree the Christmas spirit would kick in for the eight omegas and fun began.

We were allowed to put the items we made on the tree. That included ginger bread cookies, stringed popcorn, items we had cut out of paper, notes to Santa, and aluminum tinsel. Mrs. Smith had a beautiful variety of bulbs in assorted colors. The tree seemed to dance with lights were as different as the color spectrum. She placed an old red cloth around the bucket and then all the gifts went under the tree. That old bucket with the red cloth was transformed into one of the loveliest sights a young boy could ever imagine. Mrs. Smith would always buy each of us two gifts. To me she seemed rich.

We made gifts for our parents. Of course I made them for Aunt Mabel, Uncle Pug, and Smitty. One gift for mom was a cup out of clay. Our teacher showed us how to make them and then took them to a kiln to have them heated and baked. I was sure proud of my cup though it was a tad lopsided.

The Bible ladies came over and told us the Christmas story. They would put figures on a flannel board and talked of the birth of Christ. Then they invited us to their church. They were such nice ladies. One of them was very special to me in that she would always say that she had remembered me in prayer. So I reciprocated and did the same. I often wonder what happened to those angels of song and stories from yesteryear.

The last day before Christmas break was special. Mrs. Smith didn't require us to open our books. We played games such as making as many words from the word CHRISTMAS or HOLIDAY that we could. We sang Christmas Carols and practiced our parts for the play. I was usually the angel that brought the good tidings. When the light hit me, my true talents came through with only a couple of promptings by Mrs. Smith. We would make cookies shaped like snowmen, stars, reindeer, and even Santa.

I remember the first time I saw him, he entered the hallway with jingling bells and a might 'Ho Ho Ho'. On his shoulder was a big bag of toys along with fruit and nuts. Santa was here. I got so excited that Mrs. Smith had to calm me down. Come to think of it, she had to calm all of us. I sure didn't expect to see him because I thought my name was on the naughty list.

He put down his bag and with a mighty voice that sounded strangely familiar, he started calling off our names. I couldn't wait until it was my turn. I didn't have long to wait but it seemed like forever.

"Butch, come up here," Santa said. Now where had I heard that voice before? The question faded as he handed me a present. He sat me in his lap and I sure was glad that he didn't ask the question about being a good boy. I would have hated to lie to Santa. With all the skills and precision of a surgeon, I dissected that surprise package only to discover a 1955 model Buick. It was everything I wanted! How did Santa know? I looked around and all the boys had exactly what they had asked for in their letters to Santa. I couldn't wait to go home and show my family. Santa lives!

When I got home I burst through the door to show mother my newly acquired treasures. She seemed excited as well. I asked if I could show Smitty, Aunt Mabel, and Uncle Pug and she smiled, granting my wishes. I ran up the hill and knocked on the kitchen door. Aunt Mable came and opened it with a big hug for her favorite cowboy. I showed her my latest prize and she nodded in recognition. I asked where Smitty and Uncle Pug were and she told me they were gone. I thought it strange that they would be out, since one of them was always around the house. Besides this was Christmas time. She fixed me some peanut butter and crackers while she talked about her Christmas plans for us.

I listened with great anticipation knowing that once again Christmas at the lodge would be spectacular. Each year it seemed Aunt Mable outdid herself. The garland, lights, Nativity Scene under the tree and outside the house was always imposing. The other decorations around the house made me think of Santa's shop and the happiness of elves working around the clock to make children happy.

We had a Christmas ritual in which I was granted the honor of placing the special star on top of the tree. I had to either be lifted up by the men of the family and when I was older, a chair was presented to me on which to stand. I would turn to the adults with delight and feel such a sense of accomplishment, as we simply stood in awe at the tree given to us by the woods in honor of baby Jesus' birthday. Sometimes Aunt Mabel and mother would softly sing Silent Night and I would quietly wipe my eyes so the men folk wouldn't notice the tears. On occasion I think I saw them do the same but would never have asked about that special feeling inside that was owned by the individual who truly believed in Christmas and the gift of the Christ Child.

Our Christmas season began with the annual search to find that perfect tree and make it our own for that special holiday in which we celebrate Christ's birthday. One year, I believe it was nineteen fifty-six, I was asked to pick out the tree for the cabin. Our search led us through the snow until the perfect Christmas tree came into sight. We chopped it down and took it back to our home. The decoration of the tree was always a family event and so special. The rule was that we each had to make something for the tree and when we placed it upon a branch, we were to tell of a blessing we had that week.

Every year we followed the sacred family tradition of eating at the lodge, saying the traditional Christmas blessing, opening gifts, and then going to my cabin for the grand finale. The next morning was filled with laughter, joy, conversation, and play time with my newest collection of trophies. While waiting on dinner, we would sometimes go outside and build snowmen, snow angels, or snow forts. Sometimes we men would get into a snowball fight, much to the half-hearted dismay of the ladies of the house. We would come in with snow all over our coats, dust off the snow, take off our boots, and get a gentle admonishment about the weather being too cold for such antics.

At twelve o'clock, Aunt Mabel would ring the bell and announce that Christmas dinner was ready. In seconds I would have my shoes and coat on pleading with mother to let me go ahead. She always gave her consent with a nod and a smile. I would bounce out the door like a rabbit escaping the jaws of a fox. Up the hill I flew and was always the first to enter the lodge with the greeting of Merry Christmas coming from Auntie's mouth. She always hugged me and wished me a blessed day. How blessed I was to have such times of triumph in my youth before the tribulations of adulthood.

My wide-eyed wonder was evident as Aunt Mabel explained she wanted my mother and me to come up on Christmas Eve for dinner and to open presents. I gladly accepted that invitation for my mother.

I went home and played with my new-found toys until almost nine o'clock. Then I was off to bed. I remember getting on my knees offering up my prayer of, "Now I lay me down to sleep, I pray the Lord my soul to keep, if I die before I wake, I pray the Lord my soul to take". Then I offered a special prayer of thanksgiving for Santa, Mrs. Smith, and the gifts from my friends. Never once did I go to bed without praying by that twin bed for my family members and thanking God for His bounty. I was tucked in the bed by a loving mother and drifted off to a land where Uncle Pug wore a Santa suit year round.

Christmas Eve came and we went to the lodge for dinner. We were seated at the big dining room table when Smitty came in from gathering something from the barn. I saw Aunt Mabel wink at him and then said something to him. Aunt Mable insisted upon waiting on us. She had baked a turkey (mother had went up earlier and helped her fix Christmas dinner), venison, mashed potatoes, corn on the cob, cranberries, and dessert. Aunt Mabel gave tea to the grownups but insisted I drank milk. She also fixed two peanut butter and cracker sandwiches and placed them on my plate with a smile. This was our little secret sign of affection.

After dinner we went into the living room where the tree could just scarcely be seen due to the gifts. The tree was against the logs as you go up the stairs from the dining room into the living area. It had big bulbs that shined a variety of hues upon the presents waiting to be opened.

I was impatient but it was the custom to talk with each other and tell what we were thankful for during the year. I said new toys and everyone laughed except for Uncle Pug. He gave me one of those looks which meant it was time to behave. I complied with his secret code of conduct. Then the moment I had waited impatiently for arrived. We began opening all the gifts. I was amazed that everything I had asked for I had received.

Smitty and Uncle Pug stepped outside to see if it was snowing when the sound of jingle bells suddenly echoed around the house. I heard the familiar 'Ho Ho Ho' and mother looked at me and said, "Wonder who that could be". My yell caught everybody by surprise as I exclaimed, 'Santa Claus'! The sound drifted towards the kitchen and I heard Smitty yelling that Santa was breaking into the cabin. I ran into the kitchen and told him that Santa wasn't breaking in; he was going down the chimney with gifts. Silly man, didn't he know anything about the Claus?

Uncle Pug turned the outside light on and there in the snow was sleigh and reindeer tracks leading to the cabin. I begged mom to hurry but started thinking I didn't want to scare the old fellow off, so I took my time down the hill using my flashlight to follow the trail left by Santa's sleigh and the reindeer. In actuality, I was afraid that I would meet the jolly old elf and be speechless. I would rather have guessed about what he really looked like and didn't care much for the thought of seeing his belly jiggle like jelly. In addition, I was afraid of reindeer that flew.

When we entered the cabin the tree lights were glistening (we had turned them off before we went to the lodge as a fire prevention measure). Nuzzled underneath the Christmas tree that we had cut down from the glen were several gifts and the unbelievable sleigh which I wanted. It was as tall as I was and the runners were the same size as Santa's sleigh leading to the cabin.

I wondered how did he pack that in his sleigh but that old elf could work magic. After all, look at all the toys he packed in that bag of his. If that wasn't a magic trick, well nothing was. After playing with my new toys, I went to bed but sleep wouldn't come. I asked mom to knock me in the head so I could go to sleep and get up early to try out my new flyer sleigh. She didn't do as I asked but I finally did fall to sleep while waiting on the morning light.

# THE PIGGY BANK

As most children of my era, I had a piggy bank. It was a special piggy bank in that it was red, yellow, and white. It was made of plaster and quite large. I figured it could hold millions within its belly. My appointed round was to take any change and place it in the bank for my Christmas shopping. I would always be on the lookout for change that had been dropped or simply lying on a table.

When Smitty stopped by after work, he would always empty his pocket and handed me the change. I would literally run to my piggy with a squeal ("Here piggy, piggy") and deposit whatever morsels of money he gave me. I never begged, as mother would have frowned, point her finger and later insure that I would never do so again.

Whenever I went up to the lodge, Aunt Mabel would give me some change in exchange for a chore, such as taking out the garbage, and depositing in the bind so the bears couldn't get into it. I used to love to dust and wash a few windows. Uncle Pug's inspection was sometimes rough and I found myself redoing the job in order to pacify him. It always seemed like Aunt Mabel had some little tidbit activity for me to do but paid me well. I recall once I received close to fifty cents in change for simply sweeping around the front of the sidewalk and picking up sticks that had fallen in the yard. I was quickly becoming rich.

The first time I prepared for Christmas, I found myself puzzled as to how I was going to withdraw my hard earned shopping money from ole Piggy. It had a place to make a hole in the bottom of it but the money trickled out slowly. I had the bank on a blanket in the floor separating the old coins so I could put them in my combination safe. I now realize it was a toy but to me it was more secure than Fort Knox. Mother was at the cabin door talking to Uncle Pug. I must have muttered something and he asked what was wrong. I told him that I couldn't get the money out of my piggy. He stated he could and came over to the blanket. He picked it up and said it felt like it was about full. To my horror, he dropped it and piggy pieces went flying everywhere. My eyes were bigger than saucers but I dared not say anything. Uncle Pug tasseled my hair and went on his way in full confidence that he had performed a grand deed of a Scout Master.

After he left, I took a little tantrum, which resulted in tasting a little ginger tea from mother for being ungrateful. I licked my pride as I wrapped the coins. In my mind I thought of the gifts I would get everyone except Uncle Pug. He would get a lump of coal or worse. He hated helping around the kitchen so I thought an apron would do nicely. I finally got the coins wrapped and then cleaned up the pieces of piggy. I asked mother could I bury the head, which was still in tack and she granted me my request. I went to the glen and beneath my tree, I enshrined piggy's parts. Someday, I will burst Uncle Pug's piggy, I thought to myself. That will teach him!

I went shopping with the family and gathered my trophies. By that time I had forgotten about the incident with Mr. Piggy and equally shared my wealth with others. Christmas night came and we opened gifts. I got an open me first gift which turned out to be another camera with film. I was thrilled with all my gifts including the Alamo set and a Lone Ranger lunch bucket with matching thermos. The last gift I opened was from Uncle Pug. It was quite large and I opened it with great vigor. There, within the confines of a box, was the largest piggy bank I had ever seen. I was 'tickled pink', as Smitty used to say.

Each year it became a tradition that I would get my piggy bank down, Uncle Pug would come down and we would sacrifice it for the good of Christmas and the warmth of family love. Somewhere in the glen of yesteryear lays the remains of many a mangled piggy bank that taught me the lessons of love and family so many years ago while growing up in the shadows of the pines.

# THE TRACTOR PULL

Oh those wondrous days of playing in the winter wonderland of Northern Michigan! I always couldn't wait until the first snow. It meant mother going out in the virgin snow and scooping up enough of those crystal flakes to make snow cream. It meant snow angels, following animal tracks, snow forts, igloos, snow ball fights and of course, sledding.

Uncle Pug would always get his tractor out from the shed and clear the road. I loved watching the snowplow push the snow to the side. The pushed aside snow was great for building snowmen or fortifications. On occasion Uncle Pug would whistle for me and no matter where I was, I ran to him. When he was on that tractor, I knew to 'double quick' down the lane, for adventure awaited. He would hook up the old toboggan with a special piece of pipe he had rigged and attach it to the tractor. Then down the road we would go! I felt like I was flying and could feel the wind kissing my hair. We would go up and down Pine Haven Lane. My favorite time was when it was snowing and the wind was blowing.

One evening we had gone down the lane with a couple of people riding with me. It was at the edge of night and I remember the snow fading for its glistening moments in the sun. There was an aura about the land and the sky seemed to dance with color. There seemed to be the magic in the air which could bring to life Frosty the Snowman. The trees were covered with snow and I was amazed at the purity of the white and green mixture. The Reeds were frozen and I laughed thinking that the Swamp Fox had to be in his den due to the cold air and snow. Maybe he would freeze to death this winter and I would be allowed to explore the swamp in the spring.

For some reason, Uncle Pug came out of his shell and started singing. His song still resonates in my mind. They were, *"Gee it's great, just being out late, walking my baby back home. Hand in hand, over meadow and land, walking my baby back home."* I got tickled and cackled. Uncle Pug looked back in my direction and asked me what I was laughing at. I told him that we weren't walking and Aunt Mabel was home. The real reason though was I laughed due to his crooning. It sounded like a bullfrog on steroids. My laughter did nothing to discourage his off key vocalizations.

We made it back to the lodge a little after dusk and Uncle asked me to help him unhook the sled. We talked and he was in such a good mood. I think this was the first time he ever joked openly with me. We went to the lodge and Uncle Pug asked his wife to make us some hot chocolate. We sat at the 'big eating table' and talked. Aunt Mabel brought the hot coca and a special treat of chocolate chip cookies. She joined us and soon

Smitty and mother came in from the den area. Uncle Pug stood up and offered a special toast to his family and friends who were staying at the lodge. The grownups decided to play a board game and I was allowed to watch. It looked like fun but soon I lost interest. Aunt Mabel winked at me and pointed to the den. Knowing her intentions, I eagerly asked to be excused and went in to the den waiting on my playmate. I was soon joined by Aunt Mabel. She went to where she kept our cards and we played our own game of Old Maid and a card game called Snap on the coffee table. I used to get so upset when beat to a snap but always laughed at how excited Aunt Mabel became when she won.

After tiring of such activities, I snuggled next to her on the couch for one of my favorite times. They had a lamp that revolved and it had a western scene which seemed to dance at night. The lamp always pacified me and lulled me to sleep. Aunt Mabel read a story to me and before I was aware of it, I drifted into the fantasy world of dreams. I am sure that Smitty carried my worn out shell upstairs and place me in the room in the cabin that I called my own. It was a perfect ending to a perfect evening and one filled with love of family while resting in the haven of the pines.

# THE SECRET OF THE WOODS

The woods were full of animals, creatures, vermin, and legends. They were a place to be respected and were sacred to the Smiths. I remember going camping in the woods not too far from the lodge. After our duties were complete and we had eaten, we sat around the campfire. Smitty and Uncle Pug talked of wolves, bobcats, and wolverines. At dusk and into the night, campfire stories were told. I often think of a couple stories whenever I camp.

There was a legend about a black wolf that was so smart it could open a screen door. It was even said to have taken a Thanksgiving turkey off the table inside the house of an unsuspecting family. Even in my youthful age, I questioned that story. How in the world did it open the door? I had read Little Red Riding Hood and The Three Little Pigs but didn't recall a wolf opening a door. Maybe the wolf had a key I thought and laughed to myself.

The one saga that was confirmed in my mind though was about a wolverine or, as some of the locals called them, a 'skunk bear'. The reputation of a wolverine is dreadful and pound-for-pound they will go up against any animal. Most animals will run from it and even the mighty bear would give ground away when encountering this creature of legend. It is fearless, and ferocious in battle.    Skunk Bears have been known to kill animals many times its size, including a moose.

Apparently someone in the Upper Peninsula area had captured one of those fierce creatures and placed it in a fifty-five gallon barrel. They had taken the port hole off so it would be able to breathe non polluted air. They planned to have the rangers take it to a sparsely populated area the next morning and release it. Upon awakening the next morning and going to the barrel, the man noticed how quiet the captive animal was. He looked and to his shock he saw that the wolverine had chewed the porthole open to the point that it managed to escape. All that was left was some fur caught in the hole cut open by the wiry wolverine.

I thought to myself if that creature could do so much damage to an oil barrel, what would he do to a boy camping in his woods? I found myself inside the sleeping bag nestled between Smitty and Uncle Pug. I dared not get out of the bedding and even though I wanted to use the bathroom, I decided to error on the side of safety. At times I threw the bag over my head and prayed that the fire would not go out.

I remember a sleepless night and every time a twig moved, I saw the shape of looming danger; the dreaded Skunk Bear cometh! The only other sound I heard that night was a few forest creatures, a hoot owl, and the muffled laughter of Uncle Pug and Smitty. They seemed to be having fun at my expense and for the life of me I didn't understand their reasoning. Surely they were as scared as I.

# THE SWAMP FOX

(Wright Creek-The 'Reeds')

One of the stories I recall was one of necessity. I use to explore with the invincibility of a youthful warrior. I would meander down the fire lane towards Muskrat Lake. Muskrat Lake was only about four miles from the cabin and between it and my house was a large marshy area. The swamp region was known as Wright Creek (we called it the Reeds due to the willows and reeds growing in the swamp) and about a mile past the marsh was a road named after a Nancy Brown. The water from the Wright ran rapidly through the culvert. The water was filled with reeds, water plants, and was on each side of the road. It looked exceedingly spooky. I used a stick to see how deep it was and at the time I knew it would come up to my waist, neck, and over my head in spots. I never dared get in the water, though I did fantasize about cutting off the top of a car and using it to float down the bog to see where it ended. Little did I know that one day I would use car tops in the North Fork of the Kentucky River for that purpose.

One evening the boys of the Red Oak area rode their bikes to my house. We went out to play by the highway on the fire lane. I remember getting a double-dog dare from the Cousin Brothers to ride up to the swamp at the edge of dusk. They were older boys who lived in the area and I think they had dropped out of school or graduated previously. They were always picking on the 'school boys' as they called us. I was also dared not to take my old trusty side kick, Frosty, or any of my friends. The other boys gladly waited at the Pine Haven entrance. The two older Cousin boys rode their bikes to the bend just before the swamp and then instructed me to go and bring back some reeds dipped in the water to prove I had been at the edge of the dreaded swamp. I took off on my Schwinn and must admit I was scared.

You see I had been caught by Uncle Pug and Smitty once before around that area and they had told mother and Aunt Mabel about it. The next day my mother and Aunt Mabel called me up to the lodge by ringing the dinner bell and shared the following story with this youthful yet vulnerable adventurer.

The story went something like this. A few months after the Smiths bought the land to build the lodge, they were living in a streamline trailer. Uncle Pug had gone to town to get some supplies and Aunt Mabel said that for no reason the wind began to howl and before she knew it, the trailer shook. She didn't get a good look at what was shaking the trailer but she told me it was bigger than a bear and ran faster than a deer. It was dripping with water and its fur smelt fouler than a skunk. She thought it could have been a 'bear skunk' but was too big. Aunt Mabel said when her husband returned she told him about it and Uncle Pug said she had seen the legendary Swamp Fox.

Mother interjected an account of her walking down the fire lane close to Wright Creek and just as she reached to the culvert running under the road, a deer walked to the swamp and bent down for a drink. Suddenly this hairy one eyed monster jumped out of the marsh, grabbed the full grown deer and ran back into the swampiest area. She said it moved so fast that the water parted like Moses parting the Red Sea and the creature made the most mournful sounds. Its howl was the sound of a cyclone and she said it would have even petrified Paul Bunyan.

Paul Bunyan scared? They had my full attention. Both of the ladies warned me not to be down by the Wright by myself or with other kids, because

they had heard tell of children being carried off
never to be heard from again by the Swamp Fox.
Well that did it. I quickly marked that area off
my list and generalized the Swamp Fox habitat to
ANY swampy, marshy area.

Now, here I was facing a critter bigger than life,
all because of a double dare. But I had taken the
challenge and it was the sacred oath of youth. It
was my sworn duty to get the reeds and wet them
in the cold waters that ran under the culvert.
Sometimes your mouth puts more in it than it can
possibly chew.

I slowly peddled up to the area, all the while
riding in the middle of the road. In that manner I
thought that I might be able to see the thing
before it lunged out of the water and had me for
dinner. I whistled to myself in hopes of not
screaming. I turned my bike around and put it in
the lowest gear for a quick getaway. Like a good
scout, I looked in both directions and not seeing
anything bent down to reach for a cattail.

Then it happened! There was the biggest splash
and the most horrifying moan I had ever heard.
Heck with the cattail! I jumped on my beloved
bike hollering bloody murder and peddled with all
my might in the direction of home. I passed one
of the Cousin Brothers just around the first curve.
He started yelling that the Swamp Fox had taken

his brother and for me to ride for help. I was happy to oblige him.

I went for backup and got the other kids. All of them said that they had to be home because it was getting dark and left like a streak of lightning. I dared not go home and tell mother or Aunt Mabel that I had been double-dog dared into the swamp area. But that poor older boy was being carried off by the Swamp Fox.

I decided to go to the Cousins house and tell their parents about their son's demise. I rode like the wind and made it there in record time. It was getting dark when I jumped off my bike and screamed in their yard that the Swamp Fox had grabbed the man's oldest son. The father (wish I could remember his name) came to the door very distraught and told me to get in his truck. I complied. He loaded my bike in the back and off we went. I wondered why he didn't bring a gun or knife but I figured he knew what he was doing.

We got to the lane and to my surprise and relief both brothers were riding their bikes towards their house. Their father got out of the truck, pulled off his belt, cursed, and gave those two sons of his a good licking. I guess they weren't supposed to be around the creek area either. Their father told me to go home and that his boys weren't allowed up my way anymore. They must have gotten a good look at the critter and didn't want to have anything else to do with it because they never came back to visit the pine. To be honest, the 'elite eight' was relieved. The only time we saw peace from those boys was when our teacher was in the area. For some reason they were terrified of her. One glance from her and they scattered to the four winds.

I got home and due to a guilty conscious instilled in me by the adults, I told mother and Smitty about the incident. They said I needed to go up and tell Uncle Pug and Aunt Mabel about the life and death struggle. I walked up with them and noted they kept smiling but I didn't think it was a bit funny. We entered through the kitchen (back door for family-front door for guest), and walked in to the den. Mother and Smitty followed me and I was encouraged to tell my saga. As I shared the horror of the impending attack, I kept noticing the adults turning their heads as if in disbelief. On occasion one of the adults would snigger but when they saw me looking in their direction they would say they were coughing.

After I told them about the incident, they reminded me that by disobeying them, I could have been eaten alive. They looked me in the eyes and made me promise from that moment forward, anytime they mentioned an area where the Swamp Fox might be hiding, I was not to go. I gave them my solemn oath and to this day have abided by my word. Even while writing this story, I am convinced that the Swamp Fox lives on somewhere deep in the marsh. He will remain there unmolested by this believer!

(The 'Reeds' in the Morning)

# SPUD

We would go camping a lot. One of my places I vividly recall was Little Bear Lake. We would always go to a small nook away from civilization and it was our favorite spot. The water was only twenty feet from our camp and the waves would rock me asleep at night with their gentle splashing against the shore. I can still hear the Whippoorwill calling each other and the lapping of the waves, as the wind kissed the water. The Meadow Larks would offer their objections to our being there but soon realized we were not intruding upon their space. We would also build a big fire and I would fish until I was so sleepy I would have to be carried to the tent. The wind was constant and shook the trees giving an aura of holiness to the campfire. The next morning would always be one filled with splashing, catching waves and swimming up to my waist.

Early Sunday morning I was awakened by the noisy chatter of the Blue Jays. They were creating quite a disturbance about something. I got up and began walking in the direction of the dispute. I was around the water's edge and saw a little chipmunk. It was small and looked sickly. I am not sure if the Blue Jays pecked it but it seemed dazed. I caught it and took it to show my mother. It didn't try to bite me and seemed hungry. When mother saw it, her love of nature took over and she looked for something to put it in so it wouldn't be eaten by another animal. She placed it in a potato can. I decided to name it Spud. I loved that little sickly chipmunk. I took it home and did my best to feed it. It started eating a little and seemed to be recovering nicely but one morning I found it dead in its cage. I cried almost all day. When Smitty came a calling, he said we needed to have a funeral for it. We took it to my glen and buried it under the shade of the whispering pines. We buried it with full military honors. I think my foundation for honoring those who pass before me in a service was based on his respect for my feelings.

(Mother's picture was taken at Little Bear Lake in September 1956. This is where I found Spud)

# THE ALBINO

There was a wondrous legend of an albino deer that lived in the area. The story goes that it had pink eyes, reddish nose, pinkish ears, and in the winter you could not see it unless you accidently stepped upon it when it was asleep in the snow. Hunters from all over came to try to harvest it but it eluded their pursuits, much to my relief. I could not imagine anything more beautiful than an albino deer. I wondered how rare such a creation must have been. I longed to see it and I thought it should be against the law to hunt such a rare animal. I was determined to see it.

I would keep a keen eye peeled for that wondrous creature but never saw it. Each evening I would go out and watch for deer. I would sit for hours on my little platform above the forest floor but never saw anything that resembled an albino deer. But in doing so, I witnessed so many other animals of the wild that I would have missed.

On one occasion, as I was returning from a hunt of the albino, a buck (or was it an elk or moose!) got after me and I ran crying into a group of saplings strong enough to withstand his charge. He soon got discouraged and left me alone but I did not leave the area until I heard Uncle Pug and Smitty coming trying to find me. They gently scolded me but I could see the relief in their faces.

# HUNTING ANTLERS

One of our favorite past time was just after the rut when bucks dropped their antlers. It usually happened at the beginning of the New Year. On our return to school in January we would discuss it and make plans on where we would go to hunt the antlers. We always wanted to find the one with the most points. After our search, we would bring them to school and write about our hunting experiences. It was so much fun. All eight of us would try to go together and search the area.

One trip we decided to meet at Red Oak school. It was located on Kneeland Road and we walked in a southern direction towards the Au Sable River. We began the gauntlet between the two grids and looked for deer signs. For the most part, the snow had melted but the marshy area was still frozen enough for us to walk. There were patches of snow in the shaded areas and we always looked for tracks.

We started looking for deer droppings, their beds, scraps on the ground, and marks on trees from their rubs. We were taught that you could have two rubs. The first was a territorial rub during the rutting season. The other was polishing their antlers which strengthened their neck muscles and removal of the velvet. We would be on the alert for compressed leaves and Danny always

189

looked for a trail but some of the other boys didn't like to track them in that manner.

As we walked we saw tracks of a fox and decided to find its den. We searched the area but it was as if it disappeared. While looking for it, one of the boys let out a war hoop and reached down to the ground. He brought up a six point antler in mint condition. We bounded to his location in hopes of finding the other one but after extensive and exhausting search, we came to the conclusion that he didn't drop both in the area. The knowledge that first blood had been drawn with the find made us into a wolf pack on the hunt. We combed the area and were driven by the desire to get a larger antler for our trophy.

One of the other boys found a small spike of an antler and we all joked about it though we were envious. I went to the right perimeter and as I crossed a log I saw the body of a deer. I immediately imagined it was a buck but when I got to the carcass I realized it was a doe. Something had been eating from it and I yelled for the others to "come a runnin". They did and we all got spooked thinking it was a hungry bear disturbed by something from hibernating, a bobcat, mountain lion or maybe a wolverine. We decided to call off the hunt and head home.

We were close to the AuSable so we decided to walk to it and then go towards the main road. We made it to the river's edge and started walking in a westerly direction beside the meandering river. I still recall how beautiful the crystal water was and how it sparkled with the setting sun. It was then that I realized how late it was and I was three miles or more from home. I looked at Dan and he too realized how late it was. We began running because we knew that we had to go all the way back to Red Oak to retrieve our bikes.

The wind was picking up and began howling. We jumped over bushes and threw caution to the wind. It was by the bank that I lost my footing and fell into the water. The water was ice cold and I realized I had to get out of there. One of the boys cut a branch and reached it out to me. Once on the bank I started shivering. I had to keep moving but my clothes were so cold. One of the guys took off his coat and made me wear it. My bones were chilled.

We made it to the road and continued as fast as we could towards Red Oak. We almost made it to the township when a truck passed by. The boys flagged him down and told him about me being wet. The old man insisted that I get in the car and made Danny ride too. The others got in the back of the truck. We told him where our bikes were at and he stopped. The other boys lived close by and scattered to the wind. The old gentleman insisted upon taking us to the lodge.

We were grateful, as the heater in the old truck was a welcome relief to dusk's coldness. We pulled into the lodge and mother was up there looking very worried. I could also tell she was upset. Uncle Pug asked what happened and the old gentleman relayed our story to him. Uncle Pug shook his head and told his friend that he would ride with him to take Danny home. I saw that Danny was worried and knew he would be grounded for not telling his parents the exact location. Well, I guessed that I too would have to face the lecture and the fate of being grounded to the confines of the yard. My guess was accurate.

The next day I was summoned to the lodge. Aunt Mable was in the kitchen or as she called it, her favorite room. She loved to cook but this time she didn't offer me anything to drink or eat. She looked at me, patted me on the head, and pointed to the den. There sitting around the 'Talking Pole' was Smitty and Uncle Pug. With my head down, I submitted to the will of the pole and went to sit down. As usual I was met with silence before the conversation begun. I don't recall the words said but the lesson vividly remains with me today. From that moment on, anytime I was out in the woods hiking, I left a 'flight plan' and adhered to the curfew time of return. Another lesson learned.

# RUDOLPH

My favorite wild pet came to Danny and me
unexpectedly as we were coming home from
school on a cold day in January. As we negotiated
a curve in Mr. John's station wagon, we spotted a
fawn trapped in the snow. In close proximity was
its mother lying motionless. She obviously had
died from hunger and the fawn was not far
behind. Mr. Johns got out of his vehicle, went to
the mother deer to ensure that it was dead, and
caught the little deer. Mr. Johns gave it to Danny
and me to hold in our laps. We were in the back
seat as was our custom and I admit I was
frightened but the little thing was too weak to
struggle. After begging mother to let me go to
Danny's house, we took it to Mr. John's barn. He
went into his house and called the rangers. They
came out and inspected the little guy. They told
Mr. Johns that we could try to save it but in the
spring would have to let it go. We agreed to take
care of it and kept our end of the bargain. After
all we were junior rangers. Every evening that I
could, I would go over to Dan's and pet the deer.
We had named it Rudolph. It was conditioned to
come to us because we always had food for the
little fawn. It soon mended and became a big pet.
Rudolph bounded in the snow and followed us
around the fenced in area. By early spring it was
able to jump over the fence and to our amazement
hung around the area. Zip or Frosty accepted it
and never tried to chase Rudolph. Danny and I

talked about the many adventures we would have with our two dogs and deer as we rode our bikes. Rudolph would soon be able to follow us to our favorite haunts.

Late spring came and so did the rangers. They told us that we had to let the deer go in a couple of weeks and that we couldn't keep it as a pet. In fact they said we needed to let it get wild again. Mr. Johns was instructed to make it leery of humans so it would have a fighting chance in the wild. Mr. Johns told us we couldn't hand feed it anymore and that every time he saw it coming towards the corral, he would beat a pan and make it scared of people. He told us that we could not pet it anymore either and in order for it to live we would have to set it free. I was heartbroken as was Danny. Both of us loved it and wanted it to stay. As a parting gesture we decided we would tie a red ribbon around Rudolph's neck and in that manner we would recognize it whenever we saw him. We even thought about painting his nose red but were soon discouraged by the expression of the adults.

The dreaded day came of release and the rangers came. They loaded Rudolph and banged on the cage to scare it. We cried thinking they were being cruel but in reality they were trying to make if fear humans, as the area was known for its hunting season. When they left, Mr. Johns put something in his pocket. I recognized it as the red

194

ribbon we had put around Rudolph's neck. I wanted to say something but better judgment kicked in. I never mentioned it to Danny.

Now upon reflection, I realize that the rangers and Mr. Johns were right in trying to keep it from being noticed, as Rudolph might get hung up in the underbrush due to the red ribbon. Another lesson learned in the backwoods of northern Michigan. There are those moments however that, on occasion, whenever I saw a deer, I would call out softly 'Rudolph' in hopes that it would pounce into my arms and receive one last bite of an apple from my hand. That day has eluded me since that time so long ago when we saved a starving fawn from the harsh winter weather. After all these years, the little boy in me sometimes calls out to a yearling whenever one dances in a field of clover.

# BIRDS OF THE FEATHER

I think my love for birds began in Northern Michigan. I was fascinated with how these little delicate creatures could soar with such ease. I often imagined myself expanding my arms and taking flight. I tried on occasion but never succeeded in the attempt.

One of my greatest joys was getting up during the spring morning and listening to the blue jays argue amongst themselves, hearing the evening whippoorwills begging someone to whip a boy named Will, following the 'rattle tat tat' of the woodpecker drumming out a message to its neighbor, and the melodies of the little house sparrows singing their songs. I used to go out and try to see as many different birds as possible. I loved the robins returning from the south in the spring. I watched from my window as they looked for worms in our yard. I was looking at them through binoculars that Uncle Pug had loaned me when he realized my interest in birds. Before long I was hooked and became an avid birdwatcher. I think that also led to my love for photography.

My mind has faded when it comes to all the birds I was privileged to see but I do know some of their names or can describe them without too much concentration. I do remember the red wing black bird. It was a beautiful bird which had black plumage with red around its wings. Then there was a yellow bird with black wings that hailed from Baltimore. There were little black capped chickadees everywhere and on occasion I saw a hummingbird. One of the strangest birds I saw was one that imitated the call of other birds. On occasion it even sounded like a cat. Mother called it a cat bird and told me it mocked other animals. I thought it must be rude and a bully. The first time I ever saw one though made me realize it was just a little gray thing with attitude. In fact it was cute. The top of its crown was black but most of it was gray. He was a loud little fellow.

One time Danny and I were riding our bikes to fish by a small pond we had discovered. We put down our kick stands, walked about a quarter mile to this cascading water and began fishing. We noted all of the dead pine trees that had been killed years ago by a fire. We didn't have much to talk about and just sat there listening to the water meander downhill into a larger pond.

Dan was the first to notice it. A very large bird was perched in the apex of a larger dead pine tree. It had brown plumage with specks on it. It was much too big to be a chicken hawk and we both knew that a chicken hawk had red tail feathers. It was as big as an eagle but didn't have the white head or tail feathers. Before we could get a closer look at the bird, it flew off. We were excited and thought maybe it was a golden eagle.

After fishing a few more minutes, we decided to go ask Dan's dad about the bird. We went there and Mrs. John's had Campbell's soup and grilled cheese sandwiches made. She also had my favorite Kool Aide ready: Cherry. She always seemed to know when we would be arriving at her house. She called it a mother's intuition. After we ate, we asked Mr. Johns and he stated he wasn't sure but it might be a golden eagle. We got excited. Dan asked could he go with me and ask Mr. Smith. He received approval and we rode to my house. I asked mother could I go to the shop and see Uncle Pug and Smitty. She gave me permission to go but not to be a pest there. We went in the shop and they were working on a tractor. Dan described the bird we saw and asked did they know what kind we had seen. Uncle Pug thought a second and said he didn't believe it was a golden eagle because our descriptions of the bird's size were too small. Also he said in all his years he had never seen one around the area. He took off his cap, scratched his head, and simply said that it must have been a juvenile bald eagle then went back to work.

Well, first off, we didn't know what juvenile meant and we thought it must have been very rare. My thinking was that it had been bald and someway its feathers had grown back. I thought we needed to ask the wisest one of all, so I told Danny to follow me. We went to the lodge (kitchen door for family) and went inside. Aunt Mabel was baking something on the old black and white coal stove she had in the kitchen. I asked her about the bird and she said give her a few minutes and she would see what she could find out about it. In the mean time, she gave us permission to raid her cookie jar. It was always filled with her sugar cookies or chocolate chip cookies and they never once disappointed my palate. We asked for a glass of milk and I was asked to pour it. Strange, but that small token of being asked to do a simple chore made me feel so important. For some reason it made me feel closer to Auntie.

In a few moments Aunt Mabel came in with her trusty encyclopedia. She looked up golden eagles and we quickly ruled them out of the picture. She then went to American bald eagles and read about the symbol of America. When she came to a section about youthful eagles known as juveniles, she hesitated for a moment. She looked up over her glasses and showed us a picture of a juvenile bald eagle. She then asked us what we thought and we quickly reached the conclusion that we had seen an American bald eagle which was about four or five years old. That satisfied our curiosity and it also kept our eyes to the tree line whenever we were in that neck of the woods.

The rarest bird I ever saw was the Kirtland warbler. I found it so interesting because Aunt

Mabel told me it was first discovered in our little county of Oscoda, Michigan, by a man named Norman Wood. I didn't know the man. The bird was named after some doctor by the name of Kirtland who first discovered the unique species. The warbler made its nest in an area where we lived and a few other local counties but nowhere else on earth did it nest. The nest was on the ground and was underneath a jack pine. In fact I remember Uncle Pug calling them a jack pine warbler instead of a Kirtland warbler. He also said they fly all the way to some islands in the Atlantic Ocean during the winter. When I was young, I couldn't imagine how they navigated such distances.

There were places close to the house in Huron State Park where we would go to see this little six inch long bird. I remember looking at the jack pines for signs of a bird being present. On one of our outings we saw a nest on the ground but did not see the bird. I remember seeing maybe three that I recognized as males. They swiftly flew away if we made any noise. Usually we would sit for the longest time waiting on their return to the nest.

One time we went into the Huron State Park armed with binoculars and Vienna sausage. Huron State Park surrounded the lodge and it seemed to me to be the largest forest in the world. I always got excited on such excursions. I knew it was going to be a good day. We got out of the car and walked to where a sign was posted about the warblers. Quietly we made our way closer. Uncle Pug and Smitty instructed me to be very still, and if I had to move, do so in slow motion. Above all else, I was instructed not to make any sounds whatsoever, because we were really close to the nest. Uncle Pug stated that we could not touch the nest or bother it in any way because the birds might abandon the chicks.

They built a small blind made of ferns and branches and we didn't talk. That about killed me! But our efforts paid off. In a few minutes the mother bird came with worms and soon the husband came bringing home the groceries. He was beautiful. The male had a bright yellow breast with black and bluish gray feathers on its back. Its face seemed to have a mask over it. The bird also had white eye rings. It was my favorite bird because the Warbler reminded me of the Lone Ranger and I used to call it the 'warbler ranger'. I imagined riding the wind on Silver and instead of having a hawk in the sky for my eyes, I had a warbler ranger flying and guiding me towards the bad guys. Oh the imaginings of childhood was kindled in vivid colorations of imagination that would put to shame any TV or movie show!

We watched the feeding process and I noted that every time the mother or father bird came to the nest, the activity in the nest would heighten, and the chirping frenzy was at a begging level. The spring air kept the mosquitoes away and other pests that tend to ruin an outing. All was right with the world until my stomach took control.

I was hungry, so I decided to open a can of Vienna sausage and eat it with the crackers mother had packed for me. When I attempted to open the can with a can opener, the strange sound caught the warbler's attention. The birds immediately flew away and I found myself looking at two pairs of disapproving eyes. They seemed to glare at me and I was too embarrassed to say anything. I knew not only was my lunch over but also the outing. I learned that day that quiet means quiet and does not include eating on the job.

# THE ROBIN AND ITS RED BREAST

I was always target practicing with my Bear Bow
that Fred Bear had given me. I loved that thing.
I would tie a cardboard box on a string then
secure it in a tree. I would get the target
swinging, rush back to my designated spot, and
free an arrow towards its mark. I became fairly
good at that during my youth. As with anything,
I became bored and looked for other targets for
my practice arrows. I would shoot at a tree but
the arrow would either bounce off or break. I
would aim at animals but dared not to release the
arrow in fear of retribution from my all seeing
mother or other watchful adults.

I recollect that mother had gone to the store with
one of her girlfriends and I was the ward of Aunt
Mabel. Mustering all my boyhood charm I
obtained permission to go out and shoot my bow
at the target that Smitty had created out of hay.
It must have been early spring for there were
robins hopping everywhere. Robins are the state
bird and I had been told that there was a big fine
if you killed one. I would never dare kill one but
what if I simply scared it by shooting close to it.
After all I considered myself good with the bow. I
looked over my shoulder and noted that Aunt
Mabel had gone inside. There was a beauty a few
yards away. His red breast made a perfect target.

I decided that I could shoot at his feet and scare him into the air. I took careful aim and let my practice arrow fly. The arrow landed exactly where I imagined but it glanced off of a rock and to my surprise struck the poor robin in its breast. I was aghast at what I had done. I looked around and to my relief no one had seen me. I went over and the poor little thing was flapping its wings in a death roll. I was sickened when I had to pull the arrow from its body. I carried it over to the side of the hill and covered it with dirt to hide my crime against humanity.

I immediately put my bow up and moped around. Aunt Mabel rang the lunch bell and I submitted to its summons. We ate at the big table, which was usually used for guest and special occasions. We talked about the day and the beauty of spring. Aunt Mabel began talking about how fragile life was and how every little thing was God's creatures. She mentioned how important it was that we respect all wildlife and hunt only to eat. She imitated the robin's song and asked me did I know they were Michigan's state bird? Then she asked me how did my hunt go with my bow?

I was again sick at my stomach. Guilt ruled supreme. I began sweating beads as big as my marbles. My stomach churned and I told her that I didn't feel good and could I go lay down. She excused me and I went upstairs. I remember praying for forgiveness and crying myself to sleep that afternoon.

I awakened and there sitting in a chair beside my bed was Aunt Mabel. Her smile was irresistible and I had to yield the crime I committed. I poured my heart out, confessing my dastardly deed. After I told her my story, she simply said, "I know. I was watching you from the kitchen window". Then she told me a Bible verse that has stuck with me all these years. "You shall know the truth and the truth will set you free." That day being truthful was one of the greatest lessons I could have ever learned. Though I have broken that rule on many occasions since that day, the lesson is intact within the perimeters of my heart. Sometimes in life it hurts to face your worst enemy but you cannot run from the man in the mirror. He is always present.

# THE BOBCAT

I believe the most frightened I have ever been was when I went past the last cabin towards the deep forest. I think I was nine or ten years of age. Uncle Pug had warned me about the danger of going too far into the woods. My mother had also given me stern instructions on being safe and thinking about my actions before I did anything. This day though, I had my Fred Bear bow and was literally loaded for bear. Besides I had old Frosty with me. What could possibly happen?

We started walking along an old hunter's path and before I knew it, I was transformed into a woodland Indian, hunting for his tribe. Winter was coming, my village was starving and it fell upon my broad shoulders to feed those who could not hunt for themselves. Their very lives depended upon my ability to find food.

The autumn foliage danced in the wind with the colors of the spectrum. The red and golden oaks embraced in the warm sun. The hues of the fern covering the ground were orange, red, yellow and green. The white poplar or aspen with their golden round leaves slowly yielded to the call of the earth. The greenish brown of the beech trees intertwined with the foliage of the forest. The evergreens and blue cedars added a shade that words cannot express and only the eye can comprehend. This was my hunting grounds and I had to find food for the family.

The first animal I saw was a raccoon but didn't think it was big enough. I was hunting the elusive wild boar. I saw squirrel signs but it too would not feed the village. I came across turkey tracks and thought I would follow them. I might get lucky and kill two birds with one arrow!

As I walked in a swamp area, I detected the odor of something decaying. I went closer to investigate and there in a thicket was what looked like a fallen deer. I pushed some of the brush to the side, bent down to get a better look and to my horror a bobcat was staring me in the eyes. He was only a few feet away from my face. I was petrified. There was nothing I could do and I had invaded its kill. I heard its growl and noted how its ears were down as it snarled at me. I thought how beautiful an animal yet how dangerous a situation I faced. I had no clue as to how to quietly step away and dared not run for that would elicit its natural predatory instincts. Was this my time to die?

Suddenly a white streak charged past me and immediately the fight began. It was over just seconds after it started. Frosty was no match for the bobcat and soon he came back bleeding badly on his front shoulders, neck, face, and head. His efforts however thwarted the imminent attack upon me and afforded me an opportunity to escape. When I saw the condition of my pet and companion, all fear left me, I dropped my bow and tried to help my bleeding friend back to the cabin. The dog that placed his head on my lap whenever I was lying on the ground and would run to me whenever I called now needed me. That gentle creature that never attempted to growl and was so full of devotion to me desperately needed me. I was screaming at the top of my lungs. I grabbed Frosty by the collar and attempted to drag him towards the cabin. He was able to walk but was hurt very badly. I was sickened to see so much blood on his face.

Uncle Pug reached me first. Uncle Pug had been working around the mill and heard my desperate calls for help. He first thought I had been attacked, as I had blood on my clothes from trying to carry my dog. He then realized that Frosty was bleeding profusely and picked my dog up in his massive arms. He carried him up to the lodge and Aunt Mable started examining the wounds. She stated that we would have to take him to the Vet in order to save him. I was so worried. Smitty came up from out of the work-shop and took us to the Vet around Mio. After what seemed like an eternity, the Vet came out and said he would be alright but had to remain there all night.

When I got home, mother made me go up to the lodge to apologize for not listening to my elders. Aunt Mabel hugged me and said the main thing was that I had learned my lesson and that I had to be taught to follow the rules of adults. She said the woods can be unforgiving and that they were still a wilderness filled with wild animals.

I asked where Uncle Pug was and she said he went out for awhile. I went home after eating my fill of peanut butter and crackers, which were washed down with a glass of cold milk. Mother softly scolded me again but in her eyes I saw such love. Her boy was growing up and becoming a man.

The next morning I went to find Uncle Pug. I wanted to apologize to him in person and thank him for helping Frosty. He was in his workshop skinning an animal. I looked and recognized the form of a bobcat. I tried to speak but just cried. He looked at me and said that though I had disobeyed, I probably saved other animals from being killed by a mad bobcat. I embraced his forgiveness as well as his neck and that day Uncle Pug grew another six inches taller in my eyes.

# WAR OF THE ANTS

When I was alone I always played by the old logging road just a few yards away from the power lines. The tall ferns hid me from view of the road and afforded me privacy and my imaginings carried me to the battlefields. There were dozens of different size ant hills that projected out of the ground. I was fascinated with them. I liked to raid the ant hills. I would catch red ones and have them invade black ones or vice versa. At that time I didn't realize I was being cruel. I loved to watch them build their kingdoms and fight for their territory. I would take my model airplane and drop water bombs on raids to rid the world of North Koreans. One side would be my army and it depended on them whether I would return victorious or go home in defeat. The funny thing is that I seemed to always win while the poor ants were the losers.

I took my construction toys such as my bull dozer, and crane, to create highways and even used tractors to build trenches in which the war was to be fought. I even offered siege to certain hills. I found round rocks and would hit my toy soldiers. They soon became sharpshooters and would begin the battle with a hardy bang and other explosive sounds that illuminated from my mind.

One morning I was playing by the old log close to my favorite ant hills and decided to sit down. I heard a hissing noise and looked on the other side of the log. There was the first and only snake I ever saw in the area. I ran to the safety of the cabin hollering rattle snake. Uncle Pug and Smitty were in the barn and they ran out thinking I might have been bitten. I told them where it was hiding and Smitty immediately took off. Uncle Pug told me to go straight home and I could tell by his tone that it wasn't a request.

In about twenty minutes or so they returned. On the end of a stick was a big snake. They explained to me that it was a hissing viper but was not poisonous. They went on to explain to always respect snakes and keep clear of them. Uncle Pug told me that was the first snake he had ever seen since moving here. After I quit shaking, I felt pretty good as a young hunter. Heck, I was responsible for the first snake kill on Pine Haven Lodge property.

# SEASON OF THE GRASSHOPPER

Another activity I liked doing was catching grasshoppers. I remember their seasonal swarm and how I enjoyed watching them fly. They seemed magnificent in flight and the different colors of their wings mesmerized me. I asked mother if I could use a glass canning jar. She told me about the plagues that were sent against Egypt and how the grasshoppers call the Pharaoh's name to remind all regarding the foolhardiness of disobeying God. I must confess I had heard the story from the Bible School teachers but dared not interrupt mother's dialogue or I would not only NOT get the jar; I would be banished to my bedroom for the duration of daylight.

After a speech about how the grasshoppers were really locust and would spit tobacco juice on me, she gave me a jar. She also reminded me to be careful, as was her daily custom. I poked holes in the metal lid and out the door I charged. I didn't have to call for Frosty, as he always had intuitive knowledge of my location in and out of the cabin.

I went out in the yard and chased the agile flyers until I caught the ones I wanted. They would fly a few yards and then descend upon some type of green foliage. Frosty wanted to catch them too but swiftly caught on that this hunt belonged to his master and he would simply walk or run one step behind me.

I soon learned their pattern of flight and then skillfully pursued them. Once on the hunt, I was relentless. I figured out how to handle them without having their spit 'baccer' discharge on my hands. I enjoyed catching the red winged grasshoppers better than the others. I also liked the yellowish colors on some of the hoppers.

My friends and I talked about my efforts and soon we decided to use the grasshoppers for fishing bait. I couldn't allow my red winged warriors to die such a death, so I rode my bike to the dreaded 'Reeds' and released them. After carefully sorting the red winged ones into another container, I proceeded to release them. They took off in one accord but each went their separate ways. Some landed in higher hanging foliage, while others landed on reeds extremely close to the water. A few even landed in the water. To my dismay, the water around the area in which they landed became alive with frogs and some type of fish. I watched as my prizes were taken for their lunch. But in my mind's eye, they put up a gallant fight and died the warrior's death. It turned out that the yellow ones were better bait.

The remaining ones were taken on a fishing outing to the AuSable River, where we offered them up to the trout and other fish in the river.

Pending the temperature and season we had limited success. We hooked the grasshopper through the thorax and used a very thin line. We learned that size mattered. A very large one was poor while a grasshopper about one to one and one half inches was the preferred size. We used split shots for weight but were told by those old anglers that the bait had to be of the surrounding environment and not look unnatural. We did our best but never could we beat those old anglers wading in with their hip boots. Experience also matters but what a learning opportunity.

We took the ones that won the lottery and released them in an area where we thought we could catch them again but most of the time, we didn't return to that spot. It seemed for me that my yard was my kingdom and I could rid those hoppers from the house area. To be honest I think mother was a tad afraid of them. She would always wave her arms when one took flight in her direction and if one landed on her, she would make a sweep of her garments and a dash for the house. It made me feel like I was her protector.

One of the guys told me that there were places that served fried grasshoppers. He said he had eaten them and they were good. I went home and informed mother of my newly acquired knowledge regarding a delicacy. She looked at me with the strangest expression, simply shook her head, and said, "Not as long as I am the cook in this house."

Well, that didn't deter me. Someway, somehow I would taste the crispy fried critters and see for myself how good they were.

A couple of days later, I road over to Red Oak and some of the guys were playing on the field by the school. I joined in the game of "rolly bat", and afterwards we sat down to talk. Someone brought up the conversation about fried grasshoppers and chocolate covered ants. The topic heated until someone dared the youngest (his name evades my memory) to eat a live grasshopper. He was double dog dared and reluctantly complied. After a couple of crunches, he expelled the delicacy with a look of deep remorse. We all laughed.

Then the next dare came. Someone dared me to eat an ant. I protested that it was not chocolate covered and to appease me, someone gave me bubble gum. They said that the gum was the substitute for the chocolate. I protested but the peer pressure was too great, though I never did understand the logic of substituting chocolate with Bazooka but as they say, boys will be boys. I was instructed to chew the gum until it was soft and then place some ants into the gum. The rule was that they had to be living and legs wiggling.

The double dare challenge was presented and I was trapped. With reservation I chewed the gum just enough to make it soft. I was taken to an ant hill and had the honor of selecting five ants to be added to the concoction of gummy ants. The ants were red in color. I took a deep breath and then began chewing. The boys counted the number of chews and I did fairly well until I sunk my teeth into a couple of the little critters. The taste was pungent. I did not want to expel the gum but the more I chewed, the worse the taste. Then I remembered the nickname given to the ants.

Finally I could stand it no longer and I spit out the gum and undigested remains of the ants. My breath must have been terrible smelling because the taste was so bad. Everyone laughed except this fielder. I begged for relief and finally someone gave me another piece of Bazooka but this time bug free. That experience satisfied my taste for anything that crawls or flies in the insect kingdom. To this day I do not partake of any food that I feel I have to question the contents.

# SNEAKY SNAKE

I do recall another snake tale. This is one however that ended poorly for me. Danny and I had been somewhere long forgotten with his mother. I had a couple of dollars and purchased a rubber snake that was about two feet in length. I don't care much for snakes but it was a novelty and I had only seen one in the wild. I thought it would be a cute joke to pull on someone.

I remember it was in autumn and the leaves were falling all around the yard. Intertwined with the leaves were the ferns hue and the coloration of Mother Nature's splendor. I was outside and for some reason had placed the rubber snake in my pocket. I heard Danny coming and I thought quickly. I ran to the privy and placed the snake in a coiled position. He always had to use the 'John' as he called it. He would laugh because that was his last name and he thought it quite humorous. I was tired of his joke but this time was excited. He no more than got in there until he ran helter skelter out the half moon door. I laughed and once he realized it was rubberized, he too cackled.

We began playing in the yard and to be quite honest, I forgot about my newly acquired pet. All of a sudden I heard a scream and saw my mother come running out of the 'library' holding her shorts with one hand and waving the other. The men came rushing from the workshop and Smitty grabbed a shovel. He opened the door to our luxury latrine and began bashing the snake.

At first I thought I was off the hook but my heart sank when Uncle Pug picked it up and looked in our direction. I heard someone say something to the effect of did we know about the snake and I sheepishly nodded my head, acknowledging the wrath to come. I wasn't disappointed as my mother went to the sacred tree of tears. She looked at Danny and told him it was time for him to go home and I think he was more than ready to hit the trail. She grabbed me by the ear and we went inside for a little 'ginger tea'. This was a term she used for a whipping with a switch. I didn't understand where the term ginger tea originated, but fully understood the concept.

After the lesson she asked me the dreaded questions. What had I done wrong, what could I do to correct the problem and what had I learned for my meanness? I went through the torturous ritual of explaining, truly hoping for another dose of 'ginger tea'. She then had me go outside, get a shovel and bury the snake outside of the perimeters of the yard. To this day whenever I see a rubber snake I shutter and snicker at the same time.

(The old privy located at the lodge. One side was
for ladies and the other for gentlemen)

# BUG IN THE EAR

It was the season of the pests. Usually they were plentiful during July but that particular year, they were unbearable. The flies would drive you crazy and if you squashed one, it stunk to high heaven. The gnats descended in masses and were always around your face, nose, and ears. If they got into your eye, they stung. It seemed like the mosquitoes could carry off a small dog. I understood how Pharaoh must have felt! They were also seasonal but when they were out pillaging the faces and bare skin of elite eight. That was when we got the bear grease treatment. We thought that the bear grease was universal, applied to all children across the country and we became used to the smell. I am not sure what was in it but I figured it had something to do with bear innards.

It was the early morning or dusk that they were at their worst. They would swarm around us and try to invade our being with the tenacity of a warrior. Our only defense was the concoction and our bikes. We found that if we traveled at a high rate of speed, we would leave them in the dust. That was our escape route when we forgot to put on a good portion of potion.

One evening we were all out playing along the fire lane and I in my eagerness to join the fun, I had forgotten to put on Aunt Mabel's Magic

Formula on my face, neck and other exposed body parts. It was guaranteed to kill any flying object in a fifty foot radius. The mosquitoes were very unforgiving and descended in mass formation. I found myself riding at breakneck speed to avoid their feeding frenzy. I soon outdistanced them and it became a game of dodging gnats, mosquitoes and flies.

I remember looking back and talking to one of my friends when something hit me in the ear. All of a sudden, wings moved inside my ear, and whatever had flown in created a buzzing noise inside my head. To say the least, I was terrified. I couldn't figure out what was wrong. The boys rode along side me and took me to the house. I was crying and holding my ear. Danny explained that something was in my head and was hurting me. I guess Uncle Pug heard my screams from the shop and came running, with Smitty in the lead.

I was lying on the ground holding my ear and yelling at the top of my lungs. Poor Aunt Mable came to the porch and yelled something. I wouldn't let mother look in my ear until Uncle Pug gave me one of his no nonsense commands. I was still reluctant to comply and that is when Smitty grabbed my legs and Uncle Pug my arms as they rolled me over on my right side. Aunt Mabel came down and told the men to carry me inside the cabin. She turned and told the boys to go home. She got a lamp, took off the shade, and

shined it close to my ear. I still remember the
heat from the light bulb. She stated she saw
something inside my ear and told my mother to
get a pair of tweezers. She found one in her
medical supplies and brought it to Aunt Mabel.
Mother heated up some water making it warm but
not hot. Aunt Mabel instructed me to be brave
and it wouldn't hurt. She explained she was going
to give my ear a bath in warm water. I didn't
think so, but with two adult men on top of you,
well, the weight of the situation made me comply.
She took a rag and washed around my ear. Then
she poured warm water into it and held the water
in with her finger. Uncle Pug held my head. I
cried but in a few seconds the buzzing stopped.

Aunt Mabel took the tweezers and gently went
inside my ear. Slowly she pulled out a moth. It
had drowned in the warm water. She cleaned my
ear and then the men let me go. Although
sobbing, I was relieved that the thing was
removed from my body. When I looked up I saw
in the adults' eyes a sense of relief. I was
embarrassed by my shenanigans but I was
reassured by all present that if a moth big as a
tree trunk got stuck in their ears, they would have
screamed and yelled too! I laughed and cried at
the same time.

After a group hug, life returned to normal. We
went outside and enjoyed a cool glass of lemonade
while listening to the serenade of the

whippoorwills. The conversation was light hearted and the feeling of family permeated the air. On reflection, I actually believe that those terrifying moments of the moth invasion somehow made me even closer to my little family. I do recall being leery of the creepy crawly things that had wings when they gathered around my ear. Another lesson learned for life while outdoors under the shadows of those whispering pines.

# THE RACCOON-A-CORN

Sometimes legends are born out of truth and some are born out of conjecture. A few folklores are born out of sheer mischievousness and youthful vigor. The saga of the Raccoon-A-Corn was of this type of fable.

It all began when my friend and I went to Lewiston's Hardware Store. We went with Smitty and Uncle Pug. While we were waiting on the supplies, we noticed a strange looking animal on a shelf. I had never seen such a thing like that in my life. It was clearly a rabbit but it had antlers growing out of its head. The owner of the store saw us looking at it and told us it was called a jackalope. He said it was very rare and only lived close to the snipe's lair. He asked us had we ever been snipe hunting and we both shook our heads no. Danny and I didn't know what a snipe was or where such a critter like a jackalope could dwell. We asked all kinds of questions and were fully satisfied with the store keeper's explanation. On the way home, Smitty added fuel to the fire with his tales of hunting snipes and jackalopes. Uncle Pug just grinned.

We were excited about finding our latest quarry and began organizing our own hunting expedition for the spring. When I went up to the lodge I told Aunt Mabel about the new animals we had seen and heard about from the store clerk. I noted her brow forming a frown. She gently explained to me that they were simply pulling our legs. They were fabled animals and in reality the jackalope did not exist. Snipes did exist and lived in marshy areas but the hunting of one was a joke. She stated that they weren't known to be in our neck of the woods. I wanted to question her but I was fully aware that she had never lied to me or steered me wrong. I accepted her explanation.

When Smitty returned to the lodge, he was greeted by a very unhappy lady. She instructed him to refrain from pulling our legs and tell us the truth. She was not asking him but telling her offspring, as a mother instructs her son. Sheepishly he told me that he was only joking and the truth of the matter was an animal by the name of jackalope did not exist. I was actually relieved because I had full intentions of telling everyone at school about the animal and the hunting expedition we were planning for snipes, which was going to take place in the spring. After all, we lived close to a marshy region known as Wright Creek.

When I visited Danny, he too had been enlightened by the truth. We was given our usual rations and obtained permission to go out and play. We went out into his dad's workshop to get Dan's bike and go for a ride up and down the lane. Dan's father had a few stuffed animals in the workshop and had given Danny one of them. It was a very large old raggedy stuffed raccoon. He was standing on two legs and reaching out with one of his paws.

I am not sure who came up with the idea, but as boys do, we devised a new tale. What if we took the stuffed coon and stitched a stick in the middle of its head, creating a unicorn look of a raccoon? We decided to try and began looking for that perfect piece of wood. We carved and painted the wooden horn white. After repeated efforts, we managed to secure the carved wooden horn onto the raccoon. We weighted the hind legs and tied a fishing line around its neck. We were ready for the Raccoon-A-Corn's trial run.

We got up fairly early and obtained permission to go fishing. Unbeknownst to our parents, that was just a ploy for us to get into some tomfoolery. We met at our usual rendezvous and Dan had successfully managed to bring his pet coon with him. We decided that we would find the perfect location for us to hide. We found it close to the reeds. We then took the coon beside the middle of the road and placed it so the driver and passenger would see this unique animal alongside the road. Upon the vehicle's approach, we decided to rotate turns on jerking the fishing pole and make the Raccoon-A-Corn jump into the weeds. Our trial efforts proved better than we could have imagined. We were ready for the real thing and open for business.

The sun was shining brightly when our first victim came meandering over the hill. It was an old pick up and I recognized the driver though I didn't know his name. He lived in a cabin close to East Twin Lake and always wore a flannel shirt with a faded ball cap covering his retreating hairline. He smiled all the time and greeted people with a hardy hello. He was the perfect victim to our prank.

We had everything ready and at the given signal the trap was sprung. Our decoy jumped into the woods with precision and the old farmer hit his brakes and came out of that truck scratching his head. We heard him say, "Well, I swear. Never saw a coon look like that. It had a horn growing out of the middle of its face," he stated out loud but obviously to himself. We had to firmly cover our mouths so that we wouldn't cackle out loud. We knew not to laugh or it would give away our location and might be discovered. We had our prize hidden under some ferns and camouflage that we fashioned. We also had created our emergency exit plan in case someone started running in our direction.

The next car was from the Luzerne area. It was a township a few miles from Red Oak. I am sure that the old couple was going fishing because I used to see their car all the time at Little Bear and Pickerel Lake. Danny jerked the line early and

227

the car stopped. The driver rolled down his window much to the protest of his wife. She warned him that the creature might be rabid and forbade him to get out of the car. I think her words were something about that thing would eat them both if he didn't roll the window back up and get out of there. They drove away arguing and chatting about what they had witnessed. I was sure they would go to town and tell people of the newest beast in the animal kingdom.

The final vehicle of the afternoon was the mailman. He stopped at all the mail boxes along his route and we knew he was a slow driver. We decided to put the Raccoon-A-Corn in the middle of the two lane road. As soon as the mail man came within fifty yards of our creation, we pulled the line. The Raccoon-A-Corn seemed to hop and then flopped on its side. The driver peered over his steering wheel. We jerked again but to our horror the post man was out of the car and in hot pursuit of our creature. We reeled in our trophy as fast as we could and disappeared in the ferns just before he got to the edge of the road. I think this was the first time it dawned on us that someone might have a gun. I don't know if he did but it was enough to scare us off for a day. We carried our trophy back to its resting place in the workshop and hung the fishing pole on its roost.

We decided to lay low a couple of days. We listened intently to see if our legend was born.

We heard nothing and were puzzled. We talked to our other buddies at school about our latest adventure and they all wanted in on the action. We were hesitant but the temptation for mischief was too great and before you could spit twice, we were at it again. This time we had the elite eight ready for battle. We were sure that a new legend was born and that everyone was talking about the elusive Raccoon-A-Corn. We decided to move our operation closer to Red Oak so everyone would be able to participate. Plus we knew the woods well around the school area and we would be able to run through the woods if chased.

The first couple of passerby's took the bait hook, line, and sinker. We were laughing and making fun of how those unsuspecting victims gawked in amazement. One vehicle even honked for a long time in an effort to get our pet to run out of the undergrowth. We just kept a low profile while we snickered in the brush.

We became bolder and decided to put our masterpiece in the middle of the road. This time we planned on moving it slowly across the road when a vehicle came in sight. We waited for about fifteen minutes and we heard one approaching. One of the other boys was 'up to bat' and began reeling in our fearless being. To our surprise, a siren went off and flashing lights came on! The boy dropped the rod and reel with wide eyed wonder of a deer in the spotlight. He plummeted across the log we were hiding behind into the deep woods and within a flash was gone. The remaining crew looked at each other and every one of the magnificent seven took off like foxes being chased by hounds. We scattered to the four corners of the earth. We waited until the lights disappeared and the siren ended its wailing before we made a heart throbbing attempt and a mad dash to the safety of our homes. Danny and I had hidden our bikes in the ditch across from the school and when we thought it totally safe, rode the wind towards our sanctuaries.

We were very nervous and every highway sound made us think that we lowly criminals were being tracked down by those flashing lights and sirens. We went by our outpost and the Raccoon-A-Corn was nowhere to be found. Neither was the fishing pole. They must have gotten it for evidence I thought or one of the boys went back and retrieved it. I went home with dread in my heart but nothing was said about the incident and pretty soon I was outside playing with no thought of punishment.

Monday came and we all went to school. We did our usual recitations, spelling, math, and after our lunch went outside. We were summoned by the bell and went in for a special surprise guest. In about twenty minutes the door opened and a police officer came in to our class. He introduced himself and began talking about traffic accidents, bike safety and public safety. He then discussed honesty and it was then that his partner came into the school with a recognizable fishing pole. He asked did anyone know to whom who it belonged.

The youngest one of us cracked first. He began crying and pointed his fingers at all of us. Sweat dropped from my body, as the long arm of the law looked in my direction. I was the fourth to confess my sins. Finally the owner of the pole raised his hand and said he had lost it somewhere.

Then the police officer went to his car and brought back the Raccoon-A-Corn and asked had he lost it as well. I thought to myself, 'Dan boy, you are busted'. Dan cracked under the pressure and told the truth with tears streaming down his face. The officers or Mrs. Smith were not impressed or touched by his remorse. The police officers made us vow never to do anything like that again and that our parents would be notified. Mrs. Smith volunteered for that assignment with a stare that was determined to undermine any of our excuses. She wrote the note home and gave us strict orders on bringing it back signed.

I feared going home with the note. But Mrs. Smith had given the note to us with a return signature request, which meant in was our solemn duty to get it signed and bring it back on the next school day. No exceptions. She took no excuses with compassion! The consequence would be a lesson taught by the Board of Education on our behinds. Besides, I had too much respect for my teacher ever to defy her wishes.

Mother met me at the door as was her custom. I found myself not able to look her directly in the eyes. I handed her the note and she asked me where I was going. I told mother to the tree to cut a switch. She ordered me back to face her wrath.

She read the note silently and with purposeful slowness. Then she read each painful word out loud to me. Finally she gave me the note and ad me read it to her and explain my actions. Her eyes welted with tears and she asked me did I know how dangerous a stunt I had pulled. She grounded me for three weeks with only yard privileges. I was also banned from visiting Aunt Mabel and Uncle Pug unless mother was with me. The worst punishment was that I could not have any of my friends over until the prison term was lifted. It was a prank that had gone awry.

The next day in school, some of the boys talked of the paddling they received at the hands of their parents, the grounding they received and the tongue lashing by the adults. Mrs. Smith simply smiled with that all knowing look upon her face. I knew she knew what had transpired in our homes.

I was rather quiet; as my punishment was to see how much I disappointed my mother, Aunt Mabel, and the manner in which I had let everyone down. But the worst part was that I had made my mother cry. This was a hard lesson that has stayed with me over the years. Always think of the consequences of your actions prior to doing something.

# THE GHOST HOUSE

I am not sure where we heard the story about the haunted house. I do believe the sage generated from the men who gathered at the little store at Red Oak to whittle. Maybe it was the man who on occasion came out to the garage across from the school. In our youth we were susceptible to such stories. On my last visit to Red Oak, Michigan, in October 1-5, 2010, I revisited the ghost house and recalled the story of my youth.

There was a two story log cabin about a mile from Red Oak school. I remember the first time I saw it, I was riding with some friends on my bike and one of them said there's the ghost house. It sat on a knoll and had some large trees around it. I didn't see anyone around but knew that someone must live there. Folks around the area had told there were ghosts in the upstairs and if you looked at the windows long enough, you would be able to see their images passing. Once as we sat in front of the store watching an old farmer whittle, he began telling us that there was a deep well on that land and on Halloween a witch would come out of it riding her broom. She would go to the upstairs window and open it from the outside. The ghosts would come swarming like hornets and if there were any kids around, they would follow them home and haunt them. That was enough information for me to mark going around that house off my list.

Being boys of the curious nature, we would take a journey down the road towards the house. Somehow the old place came up and we mustered our combined courage and rode towards the house. We wanted to see for ourselves if any of the stories of the old men sitting on a bench whittling were true. We descended up the road with a vengeance but as we got closer, we stopped talking and whispered. The leader of the pack put his finger to his lips and stopped his bike. We hid them in the bushes and decided to go around the side of the house so we would not be detected.

Slowly with caution riding on our shoulders, we approached the house. The evening air was heavy with anticipation and there was a mist lingering from a recent downpour. Everything looked eerie and we noted that there were no birds to be seen or heard. The silence was deafening. All of a sudden a figure wearing black came from around the other side of the house. All of us saw it at the same time and we let out a conjoined scream. We were off to the races running to our bikes and praying not to be the last one to reach them. I recognized the sound of laughter and its pitch was extremely high. I thought I was in the Wizard of Oz and the Wicked Witch of the West was hot on my trail.

We took off like a streak of lightning, grabbed our bikes, and flew down the old dirt road. I peddled as fast as I could, all the while feeling something behind me getting closer and closer. I dared not look over my shoulder. All of a sudden my bike hit loose sand and I tumbled head over heels into the soft bank. I just knew I had been witched and was scared to look to see what was behind me. Suddenly it passed. The smallest one of us was paddling with all his might and passed me without looking in my direction. I was witches' bait! I got up and started running leaving the Schwinn on the highway. As far as I was concerned, the ghost and goblins could have the thing. I made it to the school and realization kicked in. My beautiful bike was now the property of that old witch or ghost. I didn't know how I was going to get it back.

I went to the store and we all started talking about what we saw. I noted that the store owners looked at each other in a funny manner and the lady turned her head trying to hide her grin. Someone mentioned I had left my bike. The store owner said he would take me back to get it, IF it was still there. I was worried to death and to be honest, quite scared. I asked my friends if they would go with me and their answer came back quickly; NO WAY!

I got into the front of the cab and though it was fall of the year, sweat was pouring down my face. I felt my stomach churning with anticipation and my fear of my beloved bike being taken down to the bowels of Hades via that dreaded well. The mile seemed to be endless but finally I saw my treasure where I had left it. Standing beside it was a man that I didn't know. I wondered what he was doing around my bike.

The storeowner pulled up and rolled down his window. He shook hands with the man and said that he had brought me back to get my bike. The man looked at me and said that I must have been one of those kids who scared his wife when she went out to hang up the laundry. He said he came running out to see why she screamed and saw a bunch of kids on bicycles heading down the road. He let out a war hoop to send them on their merry way.

So that was it! We had fallen for the oldest trick in the world. We had taken the bait of an old ghost legend by those elderly men who would be laughing at us for years. To beat it all, we had scared that poor old woman half to death though in reality she had been the one who unintentionally scared us. I really felt bad and wanted to say I was sorry but the words wouldn't come. The storeowner told him about the prank played on the Red Oak boys and the old man just shook his head grinning all the time.

The storeowner and the old man loaded my bike. The old man looked at me and said something I have never forgotten. He said, "Son, don't believe what you hear and only half of what you see". As we drove that mile long gauntlet there was an eerie silence in the cab. Finally the storeowner looked at me and said that everything was alright and no harm was done. I fought back childhood tears and looked out the window so he wouldn't see my face. We got back and I had regained my composure. The boys gathered around the truck and all of them had an inquisitive look on their face. Finally someone asked what happened. Before I could speak the storeowner began talking and stated that the nice man and woman who lived in the cabin had made sure my bike was not damaged or taken by anyone. He then told us it was time to go home. The boys looked around at each other wondering what the rest of the story was.

As we road home, I told them about the nice man and woman who lived in the ghost house. I explained that we had been the victims of a prank and that they were paying us back for all the mischief we had done. To this day I believe that a couple of those men on the bench had been victims of our infamous Raccoon-A-Corn caper. This time the young raccoons were outfoxed by the old raccoons!

# LESSONS LEARNED ALONG THE WAY

One of the lessons I learned in my youth was that of honesty. After school, Mrs. Johns drove Danny and me to the little Red Oak store to get a treat. I had enough money to buy a pop and a candy bar but not enough to get my Bazooka gum. The store owner was busy and I thought he wouldn't miss a few pieces, so I stuffed my pocket full. I paid for my pop and candy bar without incident. On the way home I stuck a piece of gum in my mouth and began chewing it. Danny asked me if he could have a piece. I gave my old buddy a couple of pieces. Never did I think that my gifts would come back to haunt me.

I went home and told mom what I had gotten with the money and went out to play before dinner. She asked me where I got the gum since she gave me only enough for the pop and snack. Being quick on my feet, I said Danny gave it to me. That seemed to pacify her.

That evening Danny rode up on his bike and we started playing in the yard. Mom rang the dinner bell and asked Dan did he want to come in and eat some soup with us. He accepted the invitation and we ate soup, peanut butter sandwiches, and washed it all down with a glass of milk. There was nothing better to me than soup and peanut butter sandwiches.

After the meal Danny asked me if I had anymore gum. Mother looked at me with the wisdom of the ages, and asked Danny didn't he give it to me. To my dismay, he said no and I knew I was busted. She told Danny it was time for him to go home. After he was out of sight, she turned and looked me straight in the eyes. I folded under her glare and confessed my sin. She shook her head, went to the walkway, and got her coat. She came back and simply said for me to get my coat.

We didn't have a car and the little store was about three to four miles away. But that did not deter that determined woman. She instructed me not to speak and to follow behind her as she walked. It was the longest walk of my life. Some folks stopped to ask if we needed a ride but she declined stating she was teaching her son a lesson. I felt as if everyone's eyes were upon her wicked son and could have crawled under a blade of grass. I might as well have been walking down the highway in my birthday suit.

We made it to the store before it closed and I was shaking with fear. I knew what was coming. Mom looked at the storekeeper and said that her son had something to say. I started crying and confessed that I had stolen some gum. The clerk said that he saw me and it was alright. Mother would have none of his logic though. She challenged his thinking immediately. She told him that on Saturday we would come back and

241

work out the gum. Mother motioned for me and with my tail between my legs; I went back in the same manner in which we had arrived. It was the edge of night upon our arrival home. Not one word had been spoken.

When we got back to the cabin, I was instructed to go straight to bed. There would be no T.V., no talking, and no good night story, or kiss. Just one of those simple terms all children dread still ring in my ear. "Go straight to your room and go to bed". That night would be filled with prayers and supplication asking for forgiveness and praying that mother would forget my actions by the dawn's early light.

The next morning I got up expecting the switch or a lecture but mother was her old self. She never mentioned my gum theft again. That Saturday I walked back to the store with mother. I swept, mopped, dusted, and stocked the shelves. After working until noon, the store keeper released me from my obligations. Mother and I started the long walk back home. This time though she talked about good things and abandoned the silent treatment. While walking along that old road to home, out of the corner of my eye, I noted mother smiling. Lesson learned.

# THE TALKING POST

There was a post in the middle of the living room. Uncle Pug had built a circular bench which engulfed the log. It had several coats of shellac on it and glistened. Aunt Mabel always had crochet pillows on the bench and I loved to sit there beside her and listen to her stories of yesteryear. I didn't care for those times that I had to sit beside Uncle Pug. He used the bench for a time of reflection and discussion, much like a time out area. This was the place for lectures and of what he called learning experiences. I recall one particular lecture that has always stuck in my mind.

The winter had been extremely harsh. We had gone out in the snow and found several dead deer that had either frozen or starved to death. It was so bad that Uncle Pug and Aunt Mabel insisted mother and I stay at the lodge. The furnace was in the basement and had octopus arms to vital areas of the house. The upstairs bedrooms had vents and the law of heat rising benefited us greatly. It was so cold that frost had formed on the inside of the downstairs windows. We even had to put blankets over the curtain and door to keep out the cold and relentless wind.

During one of the calm periods, I was to go out and put wood into the bind for emergency heat. The fire place was in the newest addition to the lodge and was used for auxiliary heat or emergencies. For some reason I did not do my chore. Instead I played in the snow.

That night the temperature dropped to almost a record low and the fuel to the furnace quit flowing. We all went into the recreation room and closed the doors, put heavy quilts over the doorway and started to build a fire. My heart sank when Uncle Pug and Smitty opened the wood bind only to find it almost empty. They looked at me and I looked at the floor. They got their jackets and went outside. I heard them dusting off the snow, opening the bind and tossing the logs inside.

The wind howled with a vengeance and the trees whispered their discontent. In about an hour they came back in with some fuel, and soaked the wet logs (I had failed to properly cover them prior to the latest round of snow) in an effort to keep the fire burning and to generate heat. They managed to build a good one and we were all instructed to go to bed on our mattresses of quilts and blankets in the floor. We slept next to the fireplace and the men took turns adding logs to the fire. The wind howled and the snow flurried outside but inside we became cozy with the abundance of covers. The fireplace sang a soothing lullaby to me and I was fascinated with the crackling and popping of the logs. The flames danced to the rhythm of the wind and before I knew it, I was fast asleep. The night was long and cold but to my relief I awakened to a day filled with the promise of warmer weather.

The men were able to get the furnace up and running by the next day. I think they had to unfreeze the fuel lines. The weather softened and broke in the next couple of days. When the house recovered from the Arctic Air, life returned to normal. It was then that I was asked to come into the parlor and sit upon the talking post. I waited for what seemed like forever. Slowly Uncle Pug walked into the living area, and slowly sat down, allowing the tension to build. He had a knack for drama. I still can see Uncle Pug's brow wrinkled with lines of disappointment. His voice was deep and rugged. There would be no tomfoolery or questions. This was a come to Jesus meeting. He talked to me sternly about responsibility and duty.

He said that if one family member doesn't pull his weight, especially in an emergency, it could jeopardize everyone. I tried not to cry, as I had disappointed one of my heroes, but the tears could not be stopped by my will power. Silence greeted the tears and for a moment I felt like my world had ended.

Then I felt that big hand on my shoulder and looked up to see Smitty's smiling face and tears streaming from Uncle Pug's eyes. Uncle said he loved me enough to discipline me and that I would lose my wood gathering privileges at the lodge for the next month. I wanted to beg but respected his judgment and feared his wrath too much to question either.

Smitty sat on the other side of me and held my quivering body. Finally he spoke and stated that someday I would remember that moment in time and come to realize that it was a learning opportunity for life. He said we all had to learn from our mistakes and once we do, we become a better individual. He smiled and stated he had messed up on many occasions too. The key was to not do it again.

As I sat there listening, it donned on me that I not only had a father figure in my life trying to guide me, but I had two. Those precious moments at the talking pole were bonding moments for the men of the family. For the first time I felt like I was evolving from a boy to a man.

We three 'men' sat for the longest time on the talking post. No words were spoken. No words were needed. It was one of those memorable moments in time.

The sound of Aunt Mabel's voice to come to the table for a meal broke the moment but not the bond. Fifty two years later, upon seeing the talking post again, I hugged it with tears welting in my eyes. For a brief moment I could have sworn I heard Aunt Mabel's stories and Uncle Pug's lessons for life in the haze. I thanked the talking pole for allowing me the honor and privilege of being a disciple in the shadows of the whispering pines.

(The Talking Post)

# THE RUNAWAY

It was another spring and I was feeling my oats about turning ten in the latter part of June. I would no longer be in the one digit age bracket but would have two under my belt. I think this encouraged my independence.

I am not sure when mother began the discussion of us visiting her brothers and sisters who lived in the eastern part of Kentucky. She stated that we could catch the Greyhound Bus and it would take us there for vacation. I was very distraught about this as I had my summer planned and it did not include a visit with relatives that I hardly knew. I protested but it fell on deaf ears. I found myself angry at the thought of leaving my sanctuary where the fishing abounded and I was free to roam wherever and whenever I wished. I was determined not to go. Mother was just as determined that I would. The battle of wills had begun.

A week prior to the trip, I became upset and put my foot down about going. I told mother that I refused to go and if she tried to make me, I would run away. She looked at me strangely and said in a very firm voice that I knew where the door was at and if I wouldn't abide by her rules to hit the highway. I ran into the bedroom and quickly got my suitcase packed with items to do just that. My Lone Ranger and Tonto was the first to be packed. I put in my beloved pair of flannel lined britches which protected me from the ticks and chiggers. I found my favorite pajamas and packed my piggy bank for the journey. I was sure that the money would sustain me for a couple of weeks and then they would be sorry for making me run away.

I put on my cowboy hat and secured my trusty Bear Bow across my shoulders so I could live off the land. I grabbed my fishing pole and rooster tails so I could catch trout to eat. I went into the living room. Mother was standing there and when she saw me, smiled at the image before her and that made me even more determined to 'hit the road'.

I remember saying that I would never speak to her again and took off up the ridge road. My objective was Red Oak School and from there to the AuSable. Aunt Mabel was working in the side yard and when she saw me, she asked what I was doing. In my fury, I poured my heart out to her. I told her that mother insisted I go with her to Kentucky for a vacation and I didn't want to leave.

She looked at me with a gaze that I shall never forget. Softly she said that my mother was the adult and knew what was best. A child must always respect his parents and though at times we don't understand the reasons, we must listen to them. I continued to argue my point as the tears welted in my eyes. Aunt Mabel hugged me and told me she loved me.

She asked me to wait in the yard. She had something for my journey. In a few minutes she came out with a pack of peanut butter sandwiches and a soda so I wouldn't get hungry. She also brought me a piece of an apple pie that she had baked for her guests. We talked for a few more minutes but I could not be persuaded to not run away from home. Aunt Mabel asked me to wait just another moment and upon her return, she was carrying a suitcase. I asked her where was she going and she replied, 'With you'. I asked her why was she running away and she smiled in her usual soft manner and simply stated, "I just can't imagine Pine Haven Lodge without you and don't believe I want to live here if you're not here with me".

I broke down in sobs and told her I didn't want her to leave Uncle Pug or Smitty. She held me for the longest time and that is when I saw mother looking through the window from inside the lodge. I wondered how long had she been there. Was she following me unbeknownst to this great hunter? When she came out of the house, I noted she had been crying. I didn't quite understand then but with years of wisdom I now realize the cause.

We all had a group hug and Aunt Mabel stated since we already had the sandwiches fixed why not go to Spencer Lake and have a picnic. She left a note for the guests and her husband. We went down to the lake and decided to go to the Twin Lake by Lewiston. It had a nice beach area and picnic tables. We stopped in Lewiston and bought a large watermelon. She called it a Crimson Sweet. All I knew is that it lived up to its name. I did a "no-no" with eating so much and had to wait for an hour before getting into the water. When I was allowed to get into the water, I was more than willing to comply with that directive. I made a wild dash for the waves. Never in the annals of history has a youthful lad splashed so much water upon the people. There were a couple of boys about my age swimming and by the time I was to leave, I had made a couple of new friends at the beach.

We left the lake around 4:00 that evening and Aunt Mabel dropped us off at the cabin. She looked at me and said she would leave her suitcase packed just in case we had to run away again. I knew that wouldn't be necessary. That evening when Smitty came in, he stopped by our house and we all talked about the Kentucky trip. Finally I realized that I was being selfish and that visiting her family was something that mother really needed to do. I reluctantly consented to the trip and Smitty stated he would drive us to the bus depot on Saturday. I did not know it at the time but the reason mother had to go to Kentucky was to sign a deed transferring the old home place at the head of Perkins Branch, in Letcher County, Kentucky, to a house owned by her brother located close to the mouth of the hollow. She was one of the heirs and in order to trade, she had to sign the deed. Sometimes one's youth gets in the way of wisdom. Mother promised me that we would only stay for a couple of weeks and then we would return to the whispering pines. She kept her word.

# THE LADY'S SLIPPER NEAR THE FORT

I use to explore the area around the lodge and try not to be seen by those within its walls. I imagined I was an explorer and was scouting the area to insure that the enemy had not detected our presence. Aunt Mabel was a worthy adversary in that she seemed to know my every move. I soon discovered a trail past the electrical lines and kept a low profile in the tall ferns. I would scout out the area around the ridge in which the lodge guarded the gateway to paradise. Those walls would be breached by me someday.

On one of my numerous outings I came across a foundation made of blocks. It was east of the lodge and had been abandoned for awhile. Apparently a house was going to be built there and for some reason the idea was abandoned. I began imagining that it was the walls of our fortification. I christened it Fort Hideout and took some of my friends to see my newest discovery. Within Fort Hideout's perimeters we would be safe; for the walls of the stronghold could not be breached in our imaginings. When some of the boys came to visit, we would sneak past the outposts and be prepared for the assault and siege to come. A couple of the guys would be the attackers and a couple would be defending the women and children within the confines of the fort. What glorious times we had!

I thought the structure was quite large and would have been a good dwelling. On one occasion I found what appeared to be wood that had been burnt. I remember hearing Aunt Mabel talk about Donna, her daughter, building a house on the property and I assumed that she was talking about the foundation. Later I heard that there had been a fire which destroyed the original lodge. To this day I am not sure which story or if either story is accurate. I do believe that the foundation was constructed by the Smiths and they knew the secrets of its history.

One time I was surveying my vast kingdom and I came across a lovely yellow flower blooming amongst the weeds next to the foundation of the fort. I thought it was beautiful. I decided to dig it up and take it to Aunt Mabel. I ran home and got a small bucket. I gathered some of the soil from around the flower then took my trophy to the lodge. Aunt Mabel was outside working on cleaning up the yard. I showed her the flower and she smiled at me. She simply loved flowers. She called this one a Moccasin flower and explained it was rare. She said it was an orchid and was also known as a Lady Slipper. She asked me where I found it and I told her. She then said she would need to go get some more dirt in order for it to be transplanted successfully.

I led the expedition and when we got there, Aunt Mabel became unusually quiet. I was going to ask her what was wrong but something told me that she needed me to be quiet for a few minutes. I excused myself and I walked around the foundation pretending to look for more orchids but kept my eyes on Auntie. She sat there for a few minutes motionless. I noted she wiped her eyes before standing and then she called for me. I ran to her with all the energy of Suzie or Frosty. She patted me on the head and told me that I had a fine play area. I wanted to protest and tell her it was a fine fort but thought I needed to simply nod my head and walk with her hand around my shoulder. To this day I am not sure why she seemed so sad but I think the flower meant more to her than I will ever know.

We went back to the lodge and she let me help her dig a hole to replant the orchid. She distributed the dirt around the roots and then watered it. She looked at me and offered me that special wink that was our little secret sign that all was right with the world. I often think of that simple pleasure and wonder what was Auntie thinking while she sat on the old foundation and why did she seem so sad? What was the purpose of the foundation and why was it abandoned? Here lies yet another unanswered question for this man who is on the road of rediscovery. But is that not what mysteries are made of?

On January 3, 2011, after a lengthy conversation with Mrs. Alys Moubry (Aunt Mabel's granddaughter), I was informed that the site I called Fort Hideout was in actuality the remains of the original Pine Haven Lodge. Apparently it burnt in the early 1940s and the Smith's lost everything. I am sure that my beloved aunt was recalling all the treasured items such as family photographs and other heirlooms that were lost in the fire. Undaunted by their loss, the Smiths regrouped and rebuilt Pine Haven Lodge on a ridge. They constructed it on a grand scale. It now stands tall against the elements as a historical beckon waiting to receive a crown.

# CAMP DOOM
## (SUMMER CAMP)

I don't know whose idea it was but it certainly wasn't mind. Someone along the way started thinking I was spending too much time alone. I protested, as I had my seven omegas and that is all I needed. My protests fell on deaf ears as I found myself being whisked away to the dreaded Summer Camp. We drove for centuries and I was the first to see the sign. It hung over the road and the words were carved into the wood. To this day I cannot recall its name. Camp Doom would have been appropriate.

I got out of the vehicle and Smitty started getting my bag of stuff. Mother tried to calm my fears but I wouldn't have any of it. Smitty reached into his pocket and tried to give me bribe money to hush my whining but I refused to take it. Now, I was a stubborn child. Those who know me will concur with my statement. Finding they could not contain my objections, they left quickly as I was now in the hands of the camp counselor. He assigned me a cabin and to my dismay I did not know one soul. On top of all that, there were girls in a couple of cabins across the road from us. This was adding insult to injury. I had never been around the fairer sex and didn't plan to start at camp.

I got the top bunk because the boy was bigger than me who wanted the bottom. He was a vulgar thing and taught me a couple of new words that cost me a lesson in eating a bar of soap by my mother. We put our clothes, tooth brush, towels and such up in a foot locker and then a bell rang. Our cabin counselor yelled that it was time to line up and the fun would soon begin. Reflecting back on his demeanor, he reminded me of a hyperactive terrier trying to please the camp director. We lined up and on the opposite side of the road were the girls. I thought to myself, this is just great, I guess we are going to have to learn to dance. They didn't know what they were facing, for the heart of the old Lone Ranger beat within the walls of my chest and there was no room for dancing. I had villains to fight and damsels to save.

We all took turns and told our names along with where we lived. We also had to come up with a nick name while at camp. I already had one and didn't want another. So they gave me one and its memory will remain within the confines of my mind. Then the director of the camp told of the week's activities. My heart pumped with anguish. A whole week at Camp Doom! I felt abandoned. That evening, after a starvation supper, we gathered around the camp fire and sung Kumbya. I thought the next thing they would try to do was to tie pink bows in our hair. My goodness didn't they know that in their presence was the son of Crazy Horse? I had no time for such dribble.

The camp director said we would be doing arts and crafts in the morning and then we would listen to stories from the counselors. It was then that I realized I had been had. I felt victimized by my own loved ones. Where was the high adventure I was promised by my family? Why was I cast out to sea without an oar? True to their word we did boring activities and silly storytelling. By lunch I knew I had to escape the quagmire before me. I was developing a plan. Maybe I could catch the chicken pox or mumps. Anything would be better than this man made torture. I would have my vengeance!

After lunch we were told we could go swimming but it rained so we listened to our cabin counselor share his life story. I often wondered if he ever got on meds for his hyperactivity. We all began to grumble. Where were the canoeing, fishing and wilderness walks we were supposed to have? Something had to be done quickly.

The next morning as I went to the privy I spotted my salvation. There hanging from a tree was Poison Ivy. I never had the pleasure of having it applied to my body and I thought it couldn't be that bad. I looked around and didn't see any one. I walked over to the tree and grabbed a hand full of those leaves, ensuring that I didn't tear a leave off so there would be no evidence of my crime. I began to administer the magic potion on my hands and arms. I thought one swipe on the side of my face would add the finishing touch.

I quickly retreated from the vine and went back to my quarters. By lunch the itching began. The potion worked better than I expected. I was in misery. The counselor called in the nurse and I was taken to the infirmary. There is where I first saw Vickie. She was on the other table with poison ivy and scratching away. She had it worse than I did. I wondered if she saw me and copied my ruse. The nurse began applying a pink potion on Vickie and I got tickled by her appearance. Then it was my turn and she started laughing at me. I think in our hearts Vickie and I knew we would be released from Satan's lair soon.

We stayed in the nurse's station with the nurse at our side and the girl on the other. It was at that location I had my first real conversation with a girl. In fact I noted butterflies. She had to be at least eight years old to attend camp. I wondered where she lived but never asked her. In about an hour her parents came in and took her home. But not before they gave the camp director a piece of their mind. Mother and Aunt Mabel arrived in another thirty minutes. I thought the director would hear it again but mother just thanked the nurse for putting that gunk on me and told me to walk out with Aunt Mabel. She asked the camp director something but I was not privy to the conversation. All I knew was that I would be departing the gateway to Camp Doom soon and good riddance.

As I got my discharge from the prison, I noted the sun shining. I witnessed the counselors getting the canoes off the racks and the life jackets ready for a cruise around the lake. I couldn't believe it. The place looked so nice in the sun and I heard one of the boys talking about going fishing after the canoeing expedition and in the evening they were going to play softball. They also mentioned a marshmellow and hot dog roast over an open camp fire. Also there was going to be a ghost roast where stories were told and experiences shared about haunts. Such stories fascinated me.

My goodness what had I done! All of a sudden I wanted to stay for the remainder of the week. The look on both adults' faces that had driven over an hour to get me made me aware that I need not even make such a suggestion. I scratched all the way home and to this day, whenever I see the three leaf venom plant I scurry away in trepidation.

My reward for my meanness was a visit to the doctor and being administered medicine all over my body that made me look like the Pink Panther. Sometimes you get what you ask for and it turns out to be totally different than you expected. Another lesson of life learned through itching and scratching.

# GARLAND GOLF COURSE

(Bridge crossing M489 at Garland Gulf Course)

A beautiful golf course was only a few miles down the road. It was known as Garland Golf Course. People from all over would come out there to hit golf balls all around the course. Danny and I would ride down there in the evenings to see the deer. They were always out in great numbers enjoying their evening dinner. I remember mother coming back from Lewiston with her girlfriends saying they had hit a deer by the golf course. Danny and I went to investigate and sure enough there was one lying beside the road. Most of the deer stayed on the other side of the large fence.

One day we went fishing but the trout weren't biting. We decided to ride down the road to Garland Golf Course and see if there were any deer grazing. We thought we might even be lucky and spot Rudolph, our pet deer.

262

When we got there, we didn't see any but there were golfers on the green. We started watching them and in a few minutes a golf ball was launched in our direction. It sailed over the fence and landed close to the road. A man walked over to the fence and asked us to get the ball. We did and he gave us fifty cents apiece. Well, our enterprising minds kicked in and we decided to go into the golf ball collecting business. Every chance we got, we would sneak away and walk around the fence perimeters looking for golf balls. When we found a couple, we would yell at the golfers and asked did they lose a ball. They would always pay us and we started making a few dollars on the side.

I guess the adults in our lives must have gotten suspicious of the new found money we had or the club might have called. At any rate we were beside the road looking for golf balls when a car honked. We turned around and it was Mr. Johns. He was not a happy camper. Mr. Johns was a quiet man of principles and put up with no foolishness. He demanded to know who gave his son permission to be beside the road four miles from the house. Danny was squirming. I was too because I knew Mr. Johns would make a bee line for my home and tell mother. He didn't disappoint my fears or expectations.

He loaded our bikes in the back of his station wagon and took me home. Mother came out and was informed of our deeds. She went to the barn and got a chain with a lock on it. She chained my bike to the hitching post so I could see it as a reminder that I was grounded for a month. I wasn't even allowed to cover it at night. Oh the humility of it all. At school Danny told me that his bike was under lock and key as well and that he was grounded to the perimeters of his yard. We didn't see much of each other for a whole month and our business went belly up. Lesson learned.

# THE CHIGGER

During my many trips into the woods, I usually went well prepared to ward off deer ticks and those red mites from the dark underworld known as chiggers. I was instructed to tuck my pant legs in my boots and to sprinkle lime from my knees down. I usually followed those directives but being a youthful lad, on occasion forgot and paid the price. Those little creatures usually covered the bottom side of certain ground foliage and if you didn't know what you were doing, you would bring home a colony and they would dig their way into your hide. The next few days you would spend scratching and itching.

It was an early summer day and the vegetation was extremely thick. The beautiful ferns called to me to come out and play. The ferns were about two feet high, two feet across and covered the forest floor with their beauty. I did put on some bear grease (a concoction that Aunt Mabel created to keep the pesky mosquitoes, gnats and flies at bay but in my hurry to play, I forgot the lime and wore tennis shoes. I walked from the cabin in a western direction to the glen. I played there and then heard the call of the wild towards the main highway (M489). The squirrels were protesting my invasion of their sanctuary and the birds yielded ground with their vocalizations. I became a Great War chief leading his warriors against the English invading the land. The ferns manifested themselves into the enemy and my trusty staff became my sword. I slew countless trespassers before one attacked me, throwing me to the ground. Slowly the light dimmed as I succumbed to the fate of all great leaders.

The lunch bell rang and I immediately abandoned my quest and returned to a babe in the woods. I went home ate a sandwich and asked if I could go play with Frosty and Suzie. I was approved for lift off and as I heard the slam of the cabin screen door, I became a World War II fighter pilot shooting down the Red Baron and proclaiming freedom for the entire world. My sidekicks were there at my side until they saw a rabbit. The chase was on! We ran and found the hole and I thought we had to capture the enemy alive and place him in the pen for interrogation. Unbeknownst to me, a rabbit always had an escape plan and our diggings proved to be unproductive. I decided to call an armistice and return to friendly soil.

I protested a bath in the wash tub and finally persuaded mother to let me just take a sponge bath. A sponge bath consisted of water in a metal bowl, heated to perfection and a wash cloth. I offered myself a lick and a promise and went to bed.

Monday morning came and I was off to the store with Uncle Pug. I kept digging and scratching on my legs to the point he asked me what was wrong. I told him I was itching around where my socks tightened on my legs. He looked at me and simply said, 'chiggers, I bet'. Well the area in the back of my knee was driving me crazy and I continued digging. When we got home I went out and played on my bike.

The next morning I felt a pain in my leg and when I started to scratch the itch, it hurt. Mother had already went up to the lodge to help Aunt Mabel with preparing the meal for some guests who were going fishing and I decided to go up there. When I started walking, I had to limp due to the pain. I had a large boil on the back of my leg where it bent and it caused me a lot of suffering. Aunt Mabel saw me limping up the hill and came out of the storage area and asked me what the problem. The storage area had a big freezer room next to the kitchen facing our cabin. Steps ran down from it and that is how we used to go to the lodge. It was the family door. To get to the kitchen you had to open the door, hang your coat on the rack, and walk past the cabinets and storage area to enter the kitchen. I stopped at the steps to rest.

Aunt Mabel met me and told me to show her my "Booboo" (OK, I admit it; she spoiled me just a tad). I rolled up my breeches and she saw the boil. She told me to sit on the steps and then she went into one of the storage coolers and brought out a piece of fatback that she cooked with her beans. She got a rag and placed the salty meat on my leg and bandaged it. I wondered what she was doing and was she going to cook me? I laughed at the thought. She told me to wear it the rest of the day. I thought that is not going to happen, but didn't protest.

Mother had been busy serving the food to the fishermen. She came out to see what was wrong. When Aunt Mabel told her she gave me explicit instructions to go sit on the bench until she came back. Busted! I wanted to explore!

I sit down like a good boy, all the while trying to figure out how to get my privileges back. The only view I had was of our cabin, the old out houses and the squirrels that mother fed who were laughing at my imprisonment. I thought to myself I will teach them to laugh at me. The next time mother feeds them I will bury the corncob. Mother had devised a holder secured to a tree to feed the squirrels. It was out of my reach but I was sure I could move a couple of loose stumps and obtain access to their feeding area.

In about a half an hour (which to a youth of eight is considered almost a life sentence), I was told to go to the cabin and mother would come down to lance the boil. I knew what that meant and I prayed that she would have to work until midnight and I would fake sleep so I would not have the operation

While I walked from the lodge and ran past the workshop, a funny thing occurred. I liken it unto a miracle. I felt a release and upon going into the house I discovered that the operation with the needle point would not have to be completed. It seems that the home remedy of Aunt Mabel's 'fat back' worked quickly and effectively. My body was purged of the nymph and the infection.

In a few minutes I went up back up to the lodge and made my announcement to all, much to the displeasure of Uncle Pug. It seems that my good news was received during dinner and he was not happy with the guests knowing of my disease. Once again Aunt Mabel came to my rescue and fixed soup with peanut butter and crackers for her favorite boy. I learned two lessons that day. One message was to always listen to the advice of my elders. That lasted for one or two days I imagine. The other was to think before I spoke and to choose the appropriate time to discuss medical conditions.

# THE 1956 SCHWINN

From the first moment I laid eyes on it, I knew that I had to have one. I was going by the department store in Lewiston and there on display in the window was the most beautiful bike I had ever seen. It was a Schwinn, black in color, with oodles of chrome heavily distributed on its frame. I begged mother to go in to the store and she reluctantly complied. I went in and drooled at the beauty of such a creation. It was a sixteen inch three speed with brakes on the handle bars. Oh how badly I wanted that bike.

Mother stated that we couldn't afford one like that but if I would start saving my money and doing odd jobs around the house, maybe, just maybe I could get one. I was determined. By the time my birthday arrived and I turned nine, I would have that bike of bikes.

When I got home I went to the barn where Uncle Pug was working. I asked him if there was anything I could do to earn some money. He said he would pay me five dollars if I would rake the leaves from the driveway island. I jumped at the chance. Well it was a bigger job than I thought but I finally finished and received my first paycheck. I helped around the house with extra chores and got an increase in my allowance to five dollars a week. Since we only drew one hundred and thirty two dollars per month from Social

Security, that amount was very generous. Within a couple of months I had saved over twenty dollars toward the bike.

Whenever someone went to Lewiston, I would beg them to go to check on my black Schwinn. Though I couldn't ride a bike, I longed to feel it under me as the wind caressed my hair. I vowed that as soon as I was able to get it, I would learn to ride. Well as time progressed, my drive to earn money waned and one day I noted the bike was gone. It was then that I realized I could never have such a prize, as I was too poor to buy it.

My ninth birthday came and mother made me a cake. She said she didn't have any money to buy me anything. I told her that was alright and offered her my piggy bank. She got teary eyed and hugged me but declined my kind offer. She asked me would I like to go for a walk up to the lodge and play with Suzie. I nodded and off we went walking in the June sun.

We went to the kitchen door as was our custom and Aunt Mabel was fixing something. She told me to go find Smitty. I went into the dining room, past the stairs and the main door to the living area. Smitty and Uncle Pug were sitting on the couch. I thought that was unusual because they were always outside working. They both grunted in recognition of my entering the room. Smitty asked me what had I been doing and what day it was. That hurt my feelings since I thought they would remember my birthday. Uncle Pug looked at Smitty and as he pointed to the opposite corner of the room said, "Son, why don't you take that old sheet off that painting I bought your mother?" Smitty looked at me and asked me if I would go remove it and tell me what I thought about the painting. I walked over hurt feelings and all, and began the laborious task of pulling the sheet off the painting.

It was then that I saw it. Though not black, there before my eye was the most beautiful green Schwinn bike I had ever seen. Somehow mother and Aunt Mabel had sneaked into the room and all in unison yelled, "Surprise"! I cried with joy. It was the best gift ever a nine year old could get. I hugged everyone's neck and bound towards the door.

I was taken outside and instructed by four adults simultaneously on how to ride a bike. Within a few seconds of mounting it, I realized that I best pay more attention to their instruction. I wavered and waddled all over the place, falling to the side and on occasion over the top. But I was persistent in my defeats. I continued the call of conquering riding the Schwinn as it was transformed into a bucking bronco. Finally I had to admit defeat for the day but I offered a solemn oath that I would one day ride the wild stallion.

The next day ingenuity kicked in when I noted the old hitching post in front of the cabin. I thought that if I mounted my bike next to the rail, I could use it to inch along until I gained my confidence. For hours I worked the rail, each time getting bolder and bolder. The day of the maiden flight came without incident. Off the railing I sailed into the unknown abyss. I wobbly rode the bike of my dreams for several yards until the wood pile next to the saw mill stopped me with a bump. I had forgotten how to use my hand brakes and plummeted into the wood. Again and again determination of Butcha the Bulldog kicked in because I knew that Danny and the boys would be coming over to see my new prize. I wanted to show them I could ride.

I am not saying that I learned to ride in one day but due to the rail hitching post, I learned quickly and soon was expanding my base of operation. Before long my skills included riding standing up, without hands (until I was caught red handed with no hands of the handlebars by Smitty), and making tighter turns. I also discovered the wondrous noise of a motorcycle. I can't say who was the first to do it but it soon caught on with every bike. We would buy Bazooka gum just to get the baseball card. We took a clothes pin and the newly acquired card and place it where it hit our spokes whenever the wheel turned. The faster we went, the louder the noise. When three or four of us road, I am sure all the wildlife in the area thought a dangerous gang of hunters were approaching and would flee into the deep woods. The sound announced our departure and arrival and we really thought we were doing something big, as we rode down the inclines to obtain more speed. We would run through five or six cards an outing and talked of patenting our invention.

My first outing came when I finally passed mother's riding abilities tests and said I could go with Danny to the old mill pond to fish. The pond was actually flowing water over a series of logs built to float them down to another mill. The trout and steelhead were always hungry. We started off and I remember how well my bike performed in the sand. A dust trail was left by our motivated peddling. When we got to the highway, I felt the pavement at my feet for the first time and knew I was king of the road. The wind brushed my hair and my heart beat with anticipation of the coming adventure. We drove down the lane to our private fishing hole and I gently laid my bike next to a tree with kickstand down. The bike didn't leave my field of vision.

I was not to be disappointed by the reception we received from the fish. They were hungry and for a moment I thought they might simply want to get a closer look at my new bike. As we fished, we talked about how lucky we were to both own a Schwinn. A good portion of my rites of passage occurred while riding that green three speed

Schwinn.  I wonder if that bicycle still exists and if so, would it remember the boy who loved it so?

(1956 Schwinn)

# THE WORLD'S LONGEST SWINGING BRIDGE

I have never seen anything like it in my life. As we approached this massive overpass, I was amazed at its expansion. The Mackinac Straits had been civilized by this five mile long suspension bridge. Mackinaw Bridge, considered being the world's longest suspension 'swinging bridge' opened on November 1, 1957. We had planned a trip to cross it but to my disappointment the opening ceremony was on Monday. Smitty said he would see what he could do about getting off of work. Somehow, he managed and we set sail for the Upper Peninsula early that Monday morning. As we approached the colossal, I was overcome with wonder and worry. I remember seeing the fresh waters of Lake Michigan and Lake Huron merging in torrents of waves and I wondered how strong the bridge really was and how good of a swimmer I was. The beauty of the blue sky and white capped waves soon mesmerized my fear. I was suspended between the earth and sky. I vowed to become an air plane pilot or deep sea diver someday. There had been so many ships lost in the straits and their bounty waited for me. I just knew that untold treasures lay at the bottom of those merging lakes and the riches were mine for the taking. That idea was short lived.

We stopped at a place to eat. We ate a dish similar to Aunt Mable's. It was called pasties. It had beef, potatoes, corn, and onions wrapped in dough. You poured hot gravy over it and it was delicious. I recall the sound of the waves and looking into the horizon. We visited a fort on one side and then a Chippewa museum on the other. I remember going to a light house on the Peninsula and then returning home that night. I couldn't wait to go back to school and tell of my adventures. All my friends were excited for me but Mrs. Smith wanted to know how I was going to make up the academic time lost. I stayed in recesses for a week and dreamed of building bridges, flying planes, and diving to the depths of the waters on my quest for bullion. During that one on one time, Mrs. Smith nurtured my dreams by sharing information she found somewhere and encouraging me to follow my dreams.

# THE HI OH SIVLER CABIN COMPANY

I believe we had lived in the cabin for two years when Uncle Pug and Smitty added on a bathroom. They also talked of building another room onto the lodge for recreation purposes. They talked of having a shuffle board area, fireplace, and areas for the guests to sit and relax. I believe it was in 1956 when they began working on the recreation room at the lodge. The bathroom project at my cabin was first though. I couldn't wait to get it installed and go to school to brag on our latest acquisition. Besides it was getting mighty cold on that 'one seater' which was just thirty yards outside of the warmth of the cabin walls.

We had to stay at the lodge during that time of construction and I was delighted. Never had I had so much room to play indoors whenever it was bad outside. Plus I had my favorite playmate available at my request: Aunt Mabel! She would take time to color with me and create things out of nothing. She was like a one woman magic show. One time she made a quarter appear out of ear. I never understood how she did that. She would play marbles with me and read to me just before bedtime. It was always like being in the Walton family, with goodnights penetrating the air. But that special tug in bed by mother or Aunt Mabel would always make me sleep better.

I also had duties at the cabin. I was the official tool fetcher and nail holder. Whenever they needed something I would go fetch it. I had to go get the lunches and bring them down for Uncle Pug and Smitty to eat.

The project didn't seem to take long. My mind's eye remembers the room having a small bathroom, wall and an area where we could put another couch. This expanded the living area quite a bit. The bathroom was eight feet by six and the couch area was approximately the same dimensions. The structure was built out of blocks and mother painted the bathroom pink. I think the other room was white to offer more light on the western section of the interior. I was so proud of our new space. I remember showing Danny how it worked. I don't think he was impressed, as he already had a couple of bathrooms in his house.

The water heater was in the corner and was gas heated like the gas stove. A few days after we moved back into the cabin the water heater caught fire. I was scared because I didn't care much for gas heat and could just see the house being blown to bits and pieces. Mother calmly turned off the main breaker, went to the glass fire extinguisher, removed it from its mount, and bravely smashed it against the fire. When Uncle Pug came down to survey the damage, he said she saved the cabin from burning down that day. I was so proud. At that moment I decided to be a fire fighter and when I went outside to play I had the worlds longest and biggest water hose fighting forest fires right beside my boss, Smokey the Bear.

I remember my first shower. It felt so good compared to the sponge bath and the once a week 'tub' bath I had to take. In the winter mother would bring the tub inside but in the summer, she would put it beside the cabin and I would bathe, all the time watching for people to appear. They never did but I did not want to be caught in such a condition. Frosty would aggravate me to death and on occasion climb into the tub with me. Mother would come out of the cabin and scold him away, all the while shaking her head at his antics. To be honest I think she thought it cute to see her two big babies taking a bath together.

The construction of the lodge's recreation room was a much larger undertaking. If memory serves, I believe the project started in late spring of 1957. I know the weather wasn't cold but on occasion we had to wear a jacket over our flannel shirts. I always wore flannel because all the other men did. I believe it was the code of the lumber jack!

I remember logs being brought in from around the land owned by the Smiths and several men assisting with the project. Norris, Uncle Pug's twin brother, was one of them. I saw other men from the area but their names escape me. I watched as log after log was put in place. I was amazed at the precision of the work and the way they seemed to know the correct angle cut.

Once the roof covered the floor and logs, the task of chinking began. It was a laborious task but it had to be done before winter. Mother had assisted on chinking our cabin (she also painted and varnished the logs) and her work found favor in Uncle Pug's eyes. She worked on what she could reach inside and out but Uncle Pug or Smitty wouldn't allow her to climb on a ladder because of the danger. I think they were over protective of her because as a child she had polio. The doctors had told her that she would be confined to a wheel chair by the time she reached her mid thirties. They didn't know the spunk or tenacity of mother though. She was never confined to a wheel chair and was blessed until her passing in 1996.

I remember what a worker my beloved aunt was too. She never complained and always possessed the most beautiful smile. She would only stop work long enough to make her family something to eat. After a long day at work, we would gather outside, bugs permitting, and enjoy a leisurely evening around a campfire close to the house. Aunt Mabel always had a treat of some kind ready to give men and lady, a term Aunt Mabel used affectionately towards my mother.

I don't recall how long it took but I do remember we worked on chinking almost all summer. I think I felt like I was an important part of the project, as once again I was appointed the official fetcher and holder. During my 'down time' I imagined I was the boss of the work crew and began wondering why I didn't start my own business. At any rate I decided then and there to build log cabins for a living and hire mother, Uncle Pug, Uncle Norris, Smitty, and Aunt Mabel to work for the 'Hi Oh Silver Cabin Company'. After all, I would pay them top wages; three dollars an hour!

(Pine Ridge Lodge's Recreation Room)

# TV ADVENTURE LAND

Mother never had to wake me up on Saturdays. I bounced out of the bed with the excitement of Christmas in my heart. The morning was devoted to cartoons. I loved watching the shenanigans of Bugs Bunny, Daffy Duck, and Elmer Fudd. There was also the Little Rascals and of course those men of mischief known as the Three Stooges! I laughed so much that my sides hurt.

The world's most famous German shepherd known as Rin Tin Tin was another show that held my attention with ease. I often thought if I had that German shepherd and the collie known as Lassie, I could fight crime through the back woods of America and my legend would spread faster than Paul Bunyan could cut down a tree. Howdy Doody, Buffalo Bob, and Clareabell always offered entertainment. I always wanted to set in the 'peanut gallery' but that wish did not materialize.

Then the height of the morning festivities was on the air. The show of all shows began with the theme that brought terror to the hearts of villains. With the mighty sounds of thundering hooves, and two six guns blazing, it was time for the Lone Ranger to ride again! Clayton Moore or Jay Silverheels never disappointed me. Oh how grand they were charging through the canyon land of the West. Tonto, his best friend, was always by his side. I too claimed Tonto as my best friend. I often thought that Danny was my Tonto but I never told him that. The Lone Ranger's creed helped mold my character and to this day I can recall the words of his creed.

The Lone Ranger's Creed
(Written by Fran Striker)

"I believe that to have a friend,
a man must be one.

That all men are created equal
and that everyone has within himself
the power to make this a better world.

That God put the firewood there
but that every man
must gather and light it himself.

In being prepared
physically, mentally, and morally
to fight when necessary
for that which is right.

That a man should make the most
of what equipment he has.

That 'This government,
of the people, by the people
and for the people'
shall live always.

That men should live by
the rule of what is best
for the greatest number.

That sooner or later...
somewhere...somehow...
we must settle with the world
and make payment for what we have taken.

That all things change but truth,
and that truth alone, lives on forever.
In my Creator, my country, my fellow man."

There were other shows I loved. Of course Lassie was a classic for all children. The Adventures of Superman kept me on the edge of my seat. I never could understand why Perry White or Lois Lane couldn't figure out that Clark Kent was in fact Superman. I would have been checking every telephone booth in Metropolis!

Sunday evening was the special time for all in that Walt Disney presented the wonderful world of Disneyland. I loved all the shows and can still recall the themes to the performances, whether it was Davy Crockett, Sleeping Beauty, or Alice in Wonderland. I can still think of Old Yeller, The Yearling, along with other classics and still get a lump in my throat. Ah, those were the days of virtuousness.

Weeknights always afforded my mind yet another adventure with the Rifle Man and on occasion classic movies like High Noon. I would sing along with the theme. 'Do not forsake me ole my darling, on this our wedding day.' I would soon be transformed into Gary Cooper facing those outlaws alone while the town trembled in fear. I would stand beside Matt Dillon in Kansas City as our guns smoked. I became Friday on Dragnet and never did I ever fail in capturing the criminal element. Jack Benny made me laugh, as did Red Skelton and Lucy. Ah, those three little channels offered such refuge during the evening hours.

The cabin had a unique antenna system. The antenna was on a pole just outside of the house and it had a control inside that could adjust the antenna to get a good reception. I was amazed by the three channels we received. How could that piece of aluminum receive moving pictures through the air and come into our living room?

The television was huge I thought. It had a nineteen inch screen and was in black and white. Mother always reminded me not to sit too close to the TV or I would go blind. My kingdom revolved around Saturday mornings and Sunday evenings. The rest of the week was my time to interpret what I had seen the Lone Ranger perform that previous weekend. All was right with the world, as my life's song sang during the summers of innocence.

# THE AGE OF ROCK AND ROLL

I think my love of music began during the times of driving around with Smitty. We would be looking around and a song would come on the radio. He would immediately burst out in song. He loved Frank Sinatra and other great crooners. He would crack me up with his rendition of Louis Armstrong's classic hits. He did a fair Perry Como and on occasion he surprised me with his Bing Crosby interpretations. They were pretty good. Now when Uncle Pug joined in that was a different matter. He possessed what I would call off key harmonics. Even Aunt Mabel would cringe with anticipation of the notes to come. She would ask him a question in the middle of a verse and though frustrated, he would forget his singing. The biggest chore I had was to not laugh out loud, for I surely would receive the wrath of a distraught mother if I did so. She believed in respecting elders and would not tolerate me laughing. In all honesty, it was funny and I always encouraged him to sing. Poor Uncle Pug, he must have been tone deaf! He did make a joyful noise though.

I recall the classics of the forties that Smitty sang. He also loved the big band music. I did not though. What impressed me most was some of the songs of the fifties. When the era of Rockabilly rushed in, I was on immediately on board with the groves. The three chord specials caught on quickly and soon all of us at school were singing along to the sounds of Chuck Berry, Buddy Holly, the Everly Brothers, Elvis Presley, and other groups putting distance between them and the era of the big band. We were "Rocking around the Clock", must to the dismay of our elders.

Then the silky smooth vocalization of Johnny Mathis and the Diamonds song, "Little Darlin", hooked me. Here was my calling! I decided then someday I would become a musician and write songs. That dream lasted for several years and it did afford me great satisfaction in playing in bands. I enjoyed playing the drums and keyboards. Though I tried, I never became proficient on a guitar and settled for learning the basic chords. My dream was to be a writer and performer. I found though that the music business was just that, a business, and I retired from playing disillusioned. Still the songs of the fifties influenced me through the sixties, seventies and into the eighties.

During recess we used to join together in singing, "It was a one-eyed, one-horned Purple People Eater" and we even drew pictures of the creature. On occasion, Mrs. Smith surprised us and joined in with the fun after recess. Those were glory days.

Then I discovered love songs. "Come Softly to Me" by the Fleetwoods would resonate through the pines, as I imagined myself singing to a damsel needing to be comforted. "Oh Donna" by Richie Valens touched my heart and though I knew females were a rare commodity in our area, I began searching for Donna. I remember "Dream Lover" by Bobby Darin, as the last song I song to the pines and aspens, which were my captured audience.

Of course there were all those glorious Christmas songs. One year one of the songs even influenced my Christmas list. The year of the Chipmunks, all I wanted was a hula hoop. I loved songs about Santa. "Here Comes Santa Clause" always made me excited. "Santa is Watching You" by ray Stevens, cracked me up and "Santa is coming to Town" made me a better boy for a few moments. My favorite Christmas songs of all were those about the Christ. How I loved "O Holy Night", "We Three Kings" and "Away in a Manger". On my winter outings, I would entertain the animals of the forest with my crooning. I am sure several deer danced just outside of my vision to the sound of "Rudolph the Red Nose Reindeer". I know I made many snowmen jolly with "Frosty, the Snowman". My Frosty would lift his ears and join in unison when I sang that song.

Some people say that you forget the importance of those formulate years. I think that locked up inside your mind is a flood of memories, as sweet and sad and the melodies we hear, which can help you to become a better person. I must say that all I am today is because of those special times and the songs which have kept me forever young at heart. In fact one of the songs that I still remember Smitty singing (and doing a great job) was entitled, "Young at Heart". Frank Sinatra introduced the song in 1953. It was written by Carolyn Leigh and Johnny Richards. Read the words and be uplifted and hear the positive message being carried on the wind.

<u>Young at Heart</u>
(Carolyn Leigh/Johnny Richards)


Fairy tales can come true
It can happen to you if you're young at heart
(young at heart)
For it's hard, you will find
To be narrow of mind if you're young at heart
(young at heart)

You can go to extremes with impossible schemes
You can laugh when your dreams fall apart at
the seams
And life gets more exciting with each passing
day
And love is either in your heart or on the way

Don't you know that it's worth

Every treasure on earth to be young at heart
(young at heart)
For as rich as you are
It's much better by far to be young at heart
(young at heart)

And if you should survive to a hundred and five
Look at all you'll derive out of bein' alive
And here is the best part, you have a head start
If you are among the very young at heart

# THE BEGINNER'S SKI SLOPE

(The remains of the ski lift built by Uncle Pug)

Uncle Pug took a notion to construct a ski slope for beginners. He talked about the design and even drew out the plans. He decided to take an axle from a vehicle with drum attached, hoist it on a platform. At the foot of the hill he put another hub, hooked some type of cable to it, and devised a pulley system so the skier would not have to walk uphill with skies. The ski lift was ingenious. He also had a motor that moved the shaft, thus moving the line. The skier would put his hand on the line and gently be pulled up the hill. I was cautioned never to be out on the hill alone and warned never to touch the cable or motor. I crossed my heart and hoped to die if I did and that sustained the promise of youth.

That fall we had to clear the underbrush and cut it right down to the roots so a person wouldn't get hurt. I enjoyed attacking the bushes that was trying to invade the lodge perimeters. I fought them with the tenacity of a tiger. Mother and Aunt Mabel would pick up the larger underbrush and pile it several yards away from the slope. They didn't want anyone to run into it when skiing or see it from the slope. Uncle Pug and Smitty used the tractors to get the bigger logs out of the area.

Soon an area was created for the beginner ski slope. To me the hill looked perfect for sledding. We waited until the first snow for skiing but once the engine was started, the lift worked beautifully. In order to see how well the lift worked with people holding on to the pulley rope, Uncle Pug had to have someone try it out before advertising his invention and lift to the public. Guess who was the first person to get to try out the ski lift? Yep, the ole Guinea Pig was elected.

I couldn't wait to the first snow but to my disappointment, sledding was off limits on the slop. I didn't have any skis so the family went out and mother bought me a set with ski boots. I was delighted because this was my first pair. I had to learn how to put my skis on and of course my first efforts were in the cabin. That turned out to be a bad plan and we quickly decided to practice putting them on outside.

The first snow covered the earth and the time had arrived when I was ready for the maiden voyage. I went up to the top of the hill and put on skis without incident. I thought I was king of the hill when I strapped them on but no sooner had I started my run down that slope when I realized my mistake. I didn't make it five feet until I tried to stop and ended up with snow for supper! Everyone laughed. They started showing me how to use my feet to do the 'snowplow' and to shift my weight. Again disaster struck. Finally after tumbling to the bottom in a series of amateur moves, it was decided that I needed to practice on flat land before trying the slope again. I could not have agreed more.

I was determined to learn how to ski and each day I was out making progress at not falling over and learning how to unbuckle the skis when I did collapse to the left, right or head over heels. Finally after several hours of practice I felt confident enough to carry my skis to the lodge and proclaim my newly found skills. We all went out to the slope, Uncle Pug fired up the lift, and as the Olympian pushed off, he could have sworn the roar of the crowd was deafening.

All went well for the first thirty or so feet but this young Olympian skier forgot to slow down using his characteristic snowplow technique. Before I knew it, once again the agony of defeat was upon me. The crowd's roar of support turned to laughter as my bruised ego was dusted off and an effort to regain my dignity. I grabbed the handle attached to the rope and to my amazement it worked beautiful. Again I won the hearts of the spectators and I felt redeemed.

After several trips, my confidence was boasted. I made it down the hill more times upon each attempt. My speed increased and I found myself feeling as if I was king of the incline. I soon became bored with the slope and I found myself wanting to go cross country skiing. I pretty much had to offer a 'flight plan' in order to get permission to go but soon my persistence prevailed.

Due to the underbrush I had to stay in the fire lanes but that was fine with me. On occasion we would go to a large hill located on the western part of Pine Haven Lodge Road. It was across M489. We could fly down that hill but our adventure was soon cut short due to the fact that the adults put their foot down because of safety issues.

Sometimes Danny or the other boys would be brought over by the parents and we would go on an imaginary adventure with our trusty 'snow dogs' to save a stranded family. The reason we called Frosty, Zip, and Suzie 'snow dogs' is that we didn't know the name of huskies at the time. All we knew was that we were those poor starving and stranded travelers' life line. It was imperative that we 'mush' to their rescue.

Our travels and adventures took us up and down the lanes. We never went too close to the Reeds though. We were warned that the Swamp Fox was always hungry in the winter. That was good enough for us but we always wondered if we could have saved those poor men, women, and children marooned in the snow covered glades. I guess we will never know what happened to them.

# THE DRIVE INN MOVIES

Oh how I loved the thought of driving to the movies. I would get so excited and could smell the popcorn all the way there. We would pull into the area, pay our fees and find that perfect location to watch the double feature. I recall that enormous screen, the previews, the cartoons, and then the main feature. The smell of popcorn permeated the air and the cherry coke was delightful. I always got a big bag of popcorn and sat next to the speaker. The speaker had to be taken off the stand and gently hung on the window of the vehicle. The sound was distorted but if you listened with all windows rolled down, the other speakers in other cars would make it sound like it wrapped around your ears. There seemed to be an endless sea of cars all pulled up next to a post that was located on an inclined man-made hill. When the sun gave up its final offering to the earth, the movie would begin. It began with previews, followed by advertisements and then my favorite part would come to life: the cartoon! The prominent event would be a movie and sometimes it might be a double feature. I don't think I ever made it through both movies prior to being lulled to sleep.

If for some reason the film broke, the cars would start honking and before long it was the sound of Canadian geese landing on Lake Huron. The honking began with one single car and then like a wave upon the ocean, swept towards the projection booth (center of the Drive Inn), crashing down with a demanding force of impatience. The sound of horns continued for the length of the unplanned intermission and only ceased when the movie resumed. Then the sea of sound would fade into the night and yield to the voices on the movie screen.

The movie which affected me most was of a Native American by the name of Crazy Horse. His vision as a boy touched me and his determination to serve his people inspired me. I cried when he was killed by his own people. It broke my young heart. To this day I remember his story and I do believe it was one of the main reasons I decided to go out amongst the people where I lived for six years. My life was deeply touched by such stories as Crazy Horse, Sitting Bull, Red Cloud, Chief Joseph, Geronimo, and other great Native American warriors. When I played cowboy and Indians, I would be an Indian unless I was the Lone Ranger on the trail of a desperado. Even then I spoke and rode with my trusty Tonto.

There was also a classic movie entitled Gone with the Wind that I adored. I fell in love with Miss Scarlett. I wanted to write her and let her know she could come live with us. She would never go hungry again. I wanted Mammy to come and live with us too. She was such a wonderful woman. I never wrote the letter but on occasion my mind wondered where they were and were they doing all right. I prayed that they would get Tara back.

I loved the ride home from the movies. I rested in the back seat with the windows down and listen to Smitty's crooning along with mother's voice humming along to the radio. Sometimes I feel like I can still hear the sounds of their voices, a tad off key, but in perfect harmony with the moment. I think that is where my musical seed was planted. My desire to play music was attuned to my inner voice of reflection upon those joyful moments, that and my being a descendent of Johann Sebastian Bach. His father and his uncles were all musicians too. In fact, the Bach family influenced music for over two hundred years and had over fifty musicians from that lineage. I was so proud when mother told me I was from the bloodline of Henry and Elizabeth Hoffman Bach, though at the time I had no clue of what that meant.

I felt the wind on my body as we traveled along the highway and headed home. The lullaby of its melody caused me to drift off into a land of milk and honey. The dreams were always sweet and the feeling of serenity pure. On occasion I would awaken to find myself secure in the arms of Smitty, as he carried me to the sanctuary of my twin bed. All was right with the world.

# SUMMER OF NINETEEN FIFTY-NINE

The end came suddenly as it had begun. It was the beginning of the summer of 1959. I don't know what happened and to this day don't understand the reason. Mother never talked about it. All I know is that Camelot was shattered.

I had just finished sixth grade and was looking forward to a grand summer of fishing, camping, and exploring with my friends. We talked of playing ball in the old school yard and Mrs. Smith had even created an eight member softball team. She had dyed shirts and matching pants for us to wear. We had to provide our own ball gloves. I got one and Smitty had wrapped a softball in it and rubbed it with oil. It was so pretty. I wasn't that good at playing and I ended up in right field. I used to get so nervous at bat but most of the time I managed to hit the ball for a single or double. I never got a home run though. Most of the time, my batting skills yielded a single. But just being with the Red Oak Rangers was enough for me. Now that wasn't our official name, as it has been lost to antiquity but it was the name I called our team.

Sometimes in your life a memory does not fade but lingers in your mind's eye. My remembrance of being informed we were going on vacation came after we had mowed the grass. We had one

of the push-type mowers that were powered by
brawn instead of an engine. The ground was flat
and we didn't have to mow that often since we
were in the shadows of the whispering pines.
Mother made some Kool-Aid and I drank it. The
flavor was cherry. I went out to play with Frosty
and Suzie by my side. We ran the gauntlet against
the bad guys, as I mounted Silver and charged
them with my trusty companion Tonto, Frosty
the wonder dog, and Suzie playing the part of
Lassie. The air was crisp and the winds from the
Great Lakes refreshed the pretending warriors. I
climbed into the fortress to survey my vast
kingdom and I felt was well with the earth.

My mother rang the dinner bell and I went back
to the cabin for dinner. She was quiet and after I
offered the blessing she began to speak. She
informed me that we were going to visit her
brothers and sisters for a few weeks. They lived
in the mountains of eastern Kentucky. I always
liked visiting because Uncle Granville promised
me that he was going to buy me a pony and I was
allowed to feed the animals. They had hogs,
chickens, a cow, and goats. In the evening hours,
just before dusk, Uncle Charlie, Arlie, and Dennis
gathered on the front porch with their banjo,
guitar, and harmonica to play. The music they
played was called Bluegrass and it had been
inspired by the early settlers of the mountain
regions. I never did understand why they called it
Bluegrass. All the grass I had ever seen was

green. I enjoyed listening and catching lightning bugs to the sounds of their music.

We packed one suitcase apiece and she began putting certain items in the attic. I thought that odd, since we never did put things up there when we went on a trip. I remember her cleaning the cabin and how nice it looked. My toys were all organized in neat rolls and I had my prized possessions guarding the Alamo set I had. The Lone Ranger, Tonto, Silver, and Scout set on the top shelves in all the splendor and majesty of their character daring anyone to touch the sacred items left behind. Mother put her guitar in the attic for 'safe keeping' and told me to make sure all my clothes were in the dresser. I was happy to do so, knowing upon our return we would not have to pick up things in the house.

I was excited about the trip and the next day when Danny came over, I bragged about riding on a bus and going around the mountain to the top to visit my kinfolk. Dan looked sad and disappointed. We both brushed it off and we rode our bikes to the AuSable River with fishing gear in tow. As we had done on so many occasions, we cast our lines upon the pristine water. Little did I know that this would be the last time I would see my best friend or fish the mighty AuSable River.

The next morning Smitty took us to the Greyhound bus station in Grayling. The drive to

Grayling was a solemn one with the conversation being pleasant, yet as I reflect upon that day, there seemed to be tension in the air. I still do not know why and maybe it was my over abundance of imagination that still haunts me this day. Smitty pointed out some of the majestic exquisiteness of the land and told me to always remember the beauty of the back woods. I bet I saw twenty deer that morning and I am sure I saw a red fox dart across the road. Between the main road and the lodge, there lived a fox family. I loved watching the kits play when I was perched a few feet above the ground in my make-shift blind. The fox squirrels scurried up and down the tree line as if they were paying tribute to me for feeding them on so many occasions.

Then it hit me! Frosty, I had forgotten about my dog. Of course on those occasions I had to forbid Frosty from accompanying me. Besides they didn't allow dogs to ride a bus. My mind rushed to Frosty. Who would take care of him while I was away from home? Then I thought of Smitty. I asked Smitty would he take good care of my beloved pet. He said he would treat him like he was his own dog. That afforded me great comfort. I also had two gold fish named Sylvester and Tweety. One was black the other gold. Smitty promised to feed them every day and make sure the water was changed. I knew they were in good hands with Smitty, my 'bestest' of friends.

My excitement built as we arrived at our destination. The station seemed so large to me and the smell of diesel fuel permeated the air. Mother went to the counter, purchased the tickets, and pointed to our bus. The bus was a double decker and I was so impressed. This was the fanciest bus I had ever seen. I couldn't wait to get on it and start pushing buttons on the seat.

I was puzzled by the manner in which Smitty said goodbye. He broke down, sobbing with unabated tears streaming down his face, and hugged me as if this would be the last time he would ever see me. I had never seen a grown man cry before and I felt such pity for him. In hopes of making him 'Smiling Smitty' again, I told him we would be back in a couple of weeks. I told him that I loved him and to tell Aunt Mabel and Uncle Pug that I loved them too. I couldn't figure out why they didn't come with us to see their boy off on another adventure. I guess they must have had guests and couldn't get away. Mother didn't say anything.

The announcement came that our bus was departing. We said our tearful goodbyes. Smitty held mother for the longest time and gently kissed her check. Then he grabbed "his boy" in his arms and swung me around in a circle like was his custom. He patted me on the head and said something I shall never forget. He looked me in the square in the eyes and said, "Never forget the days of the whispering pines".

We got on the bus and to my delight we were in the top section of the bus. The bus backed up and I waved at Smitty with the biggest grin upon my face. His wave seemed half-hearted but I could not grasp the reason. Nothing could pull me away from my cabin. We started heading out of the terminal and with my last glimpse I saw Smitty standing beside the loading area all alone. That was the first time I ever noticed a person looking fragile, forlorn, and afraid. There seemed to be panic in his continence. His eyes were consumed with unabated tears of sorrow. Had I done something wrong? Why was he crying?

All of a sudden I had a deep longing to stay. I wanted him to be beside me on my latest adventure. I wanted him to run to the bus and get on with us. I looked at mother who seemed so sad too. Had I missed something? We would be a family again in only a couple of weeks so why the long faces? When I returned I would show him how much he really meant to me. His image faded as we gained momentum, and soon he disappeared in the horizon. That was the last time that I ever saw Smitty and though my memory of a time long ago has been dimmed by the advancement of age, his stature in my eyes has grown through the years.

# REVISITING CAMELOT

On a voyage that has taken over fifty-two years to complete, I discovered many facts and figures. Most of what I unearthed was about me facing a forgotten era and chapter in my life. More importantly I rekindled such deep emotions during my quest. Sometimes I would simply stand in the doorway of the cabin and yield a cry of longing. Sometimes I would walk and hear Frosty's bark in the distance. Occasionally I felt the presence of the Lone Ranger and Tonto guiding my reflections. From time to time I could not contain myself in the tears and the laughter for days long ago. It was the sweetest sorrow of rediscovery I have ever known.

Morris A. Smith's last known residence was Route 2, Box 65, Mio, Michigan. His Social Security number was 379-07-1374. Uncle Pug died on December 06, 1973, due to a massive heart attack. He was eighty-two at his passing and he died without knowing the impact he had upon this fielder. He is buried in Flint Memorial Park, Flint, Michigan, (located on 9506 N. Dort Street, Mt. Morris) Genesee County, in section R, Lot 95, Plots 6 & 8. I visited the location and placed a small flower and tears of gratitude upon his grave.

Uncle Pug is buried in the military section of the cemetery close to the North Gate and the

Information Center. They are resting under the shade of a grand tree. His twin brother, Norris C. Smith, is buried at his feet. His stone simply states, Norris C. 1891-1963. Norris's wife, Myrtle B., is buried to Norris's left. Her stone reads Myrtle B., 1892-1958. Uncle Pug's stone inscription simply states the following:

M A Smith,
Mich
MM1
U S Navy
WWI
9/4/91-12/6/73

(Special thanks to Mio, Michigan County Court Clerk-Becky Smutek & Thelma Miller, Family Service Counselor, of Flint Memorial Park for their invaluable assistance).

Uncle Pug never talked to me about his service during World War One. Being unsure of the responsibilities and a MM1, I decided to research it. I found a simplified explanation via Wikipedia. The following definition was offered: *"According to the United States Navy Bureau of Naval Personnel (BUPERS), the job of an MM is to 'operate, maintain, and repair (organizational and intermediate level) ship propulsion machinery, auxiliary equipment, and outside machinery, such as: steering engine, hoisting machinery, food preparation equipment, refrigeration and air conditioning equipment, windlasses, elevators,* and laundry equipment. Operate and maintain (organizational and intermediate level) marine boilers, pumps, forced draft blowers, and heat exchangers; perform tests, transfers, and inventory of lubricating oils, fuels, and water. Maintain records and reports, and may perform duties in the generation and stowage of industrial gases.' Enlistees are taught the fundamentals of this rating through on-the-job training or formal Navy schooling." Uncle Pug's service during World War I entailed being inside the working mechanics of the ship to ensure it functioned properly throughout the voyage.

On October 1, 2010, I once again revisited Doug and Suzan at Pine Ridge Lodge to continue my quest. I found myself meandering in the area in search of anyone who remembered Uncle Pug, Aunt Mable and Smitty. I drove to Lewiston, Michigan, where I distributed flyers to the Senior Citizen building and local businesses. I went to McKinley and Mio and talked to several locals. I placed flyers in that area regarding the whereabouts of those I sought.

On October 22, 2010, I received a letter from Karen Sue Smith of Mio, Michigan. She stated that she is the niece of Mike Allan Smith, Mrs. Marie Smith's husband. In the letter she gave me insightful information about my former teacher. She stated that, "Marie died several years ago after a long and much fulfilled life! Aunt Marie's maiden name was Galbraith." Ms. Karen suggested I contact some of that family. They own State Wide Real Estate and their son owns AuSable River Restaurant where I left a flyer that Ms. Karen found! God works in mysterious ways.

She also suggested I contact Mio AuSable School, as they hold an Alumni Banquet every year (1st week of October)! Ironically I was there on that date and talked to Central Office located inside the school, but they did not mention the banquet). I was ecstatic with joy and found her letters were covered with tears of gratitude.

On November 3, 2010, I once again talked to Miss Thelma Miller regarding the unmarked plot number six (6) adjacent to Uncle Pug. She reviewed her records and confirmed that Aunt Mabel is not buried beside of Uncle Pug, though the plot is available for a memorial marker. Mrs. Thelma Miller continued to review the cemetery records and called me back later that day. She stated that she could not find Aunt Mabel's name listed as being buried in the Flint Memorial Cemetery. Though disappointed, I remained determined and committed in my quest for this wonderful lady.

The last known Smith to visit the lodge was Alys Moubry, whose address at the time of her visit was in Colorado. She visited the lodge in the year nineteen-ninety five.

On Wednesday, November 17, 2010, I received a letter that brought tears of sadness and of joy to my eyes. The letter was from Mrs. Margaret Smith Hodge, the daughter of my former teacher. The three page letter contained invaluable information regarding Mrs. Marie Smith. Mrs. Hodge stated that her, *"Mom died February 7, 2002. It was a remarkable funeral. She passed away in Florida, and I thought maybe a few people would show up for a memorial there, but the place was full. Then we had a memorial at Mio Church of God. The minister had prepared a sermon, but he first asked if anyone wanted to say a few words. Person after person stood up and talked and after almost an hour, the minister said, 'Well, I can't top that, so let's just sing a song'. Then I decided to bury her ashes (Kettle Cemetery is located about three miles north approximately two miles west of Mio) on her birthday (April 21). I am so amazed that she had such an impact on so many people. Everyone she met can be assured that they were loved by someone."*

In her letter she stated that her mother kept a diary all her life. I can only imagine what is written within its pages. Before Mrs. Hodge closed, she shared a story that captured the very essence of Mrs. Marie Smith's character. I offer it verbatim for the reader. *"I just have to share one story before closing. Mom's last years were spent at the Barney Park Apartments in Fairview. While there she was talking with a old gentlemen and he said his one regret was never learning to read or write, as he was so busy feeding and clothing a large family and working in the factories. Mom made some flash cards and taught a ninety+ man to read and write. He wrote his daughter a letter before he died and it was a highlight for both of them. When mom retired from teaching, she got letters from President Nixon and Governor Milliken. I have them. Walking in those shoes is an impossible task, but growing up with all the confidence I needed was such a blessing."*

On November 20, 2010, I received an email from Mrs. Hodges. In her correspondence she stated that she had been reading her mother's diary and had found some interesting tidbits regarding her. I wish to share them in an effort to demonstrate the impact Mrs. Marie Smith had on others. *"I did run across the name Gilbert Cordell in the diary. Hank was special to our family...for whatever reason...just a cute kid, I guess. He grew into a very handsome man and still sweet natured. I can't wait to share some of these writing with you. Do you remember the Kahn boys? One of them was, and maybe still is, Sheriff of Oscoda County. I remember several years ago Mom and I were walking down the sidewalk in Mio and a big man ran up and grabbed Mom and swung her around...I was shocked! She was giggling...it was one of the Kahn boys she had taught at Red Oak. He was clearly glad to see her! I don't remember the details, but I think there was a Cordell girl, and it seems Mom was so glad because she got honors when she went to Mio, and that had never happened to a student from Red Oak before. M"*

Mrs. Marie's diaries are a treasure of information regarding the past and I can't wait to obtain a copy once Mrs. Hodge has them published. I wish to share another tidbit as enticement and appetizer for your curiosity. Regarding the salary in those days, Mrs. Marie Smith made the following entry: Note the pay salary in 1957. *"April 17, 1957....Mike and I went up to school & I signed contract for next year...$3,060.00 for nine months. $170.00 every two weeks. I enjoyed this year."*

After reading her letter and emails, I wondered how many lives Marie Smith had touched and what her impact on others was. I can only tell the reader that her efforts in and out of the classroom strengthened me and gave me a burning desire to better myself so future generations would wish to grasp the torch of enlightenment with a lover's embrace. Though she is gone, as is Uncle Pug, Aunt Mable, Smitty, and countless others who nurtured me, their legacy continues to this day to be shared through me. It is said that the greatest gifts are those you give away. While nestled in the shadows of the whispering pines, everyone in my life was my teacher, a mentor, and gave me gifts that I will never be able to duplicate.

As I had mentioned previously, I received a phone call from Alys Moubry, the solitary grandchild of Morris and Mabel Smith. We both were delighted to have made contact and her information confirmed my reflections and complimented my endeavors at capturing those moments. She also revitalized my efforts towards leaving a legacy for the family, community, and that particular era. Sometimes we would get so over-zealous in our conversation that we would finish each other's statement. Then there were those moments in which we felt an involuntary sob come from our throats in remembrance of a by-gone epoch.

As we talked, she brought back the memory of Uncle Pug and Aunt Mabel's Bridge playing abilities. They were avid players and were noted state-wide. Their dearest friends (I had forgotten their names until Alys stated them), Ken and Pat Valentine, would visit them and they would play for hours together. On occasion they would go to Bridge Tournaments and returned as the winners on most occasions. Also they were proficient in a card game called Pinochle. The game is played with forty-eight cards and four people, with one being the dealer. Then they bid for points they expect to win. That is about the extent of my poor knowledge on the card game. I was never interested in cards due to my father's gambling habits and the final results of his demise.

A memory that Alys vividly recalled was that of Aunt Mabel using the wringer-washer washing machine and then hanging up the clothes outside to dry. That image triggered seeing my mother doing the same when at the lodge on laundry day. I remember handing them the clothes pins and feeling the wind, as it shook the clothes in a joint effort with the sun to dry them. I also remembered mother and Aunt Mabel running to the clothes and getting them off the line before the rain came or the wind blew them to another county.

There was also a time with I was fascinated with the wringer on the washer and wondered if it would flatten my fingers. I tried and I cried. Both mother and Aunt Mabel ran and one of them turned the release on top of the wringer-washing machine (I believe the name of the washing machine was Speed Queen). I was more frightened than hurt but there was a valuable lesson learned on that day. Don't go sticking your hands where they don't belong. Funny how such little things mean so much in our later years.

Alys also mentioned that whenever it snowed, her grandfather would get out the old tractor from the garage and plow the lane. He would always pile the snow in one spot and that became the play area. As soon as she talked about that, I couldn't help but chuckle. I too used the snow as a ski slope. I didn't have any skis then, so I would cut a box open and slide down the slope on it. Sometimes I would have an inner tube that we patched for that purpose. We also played King of the Hill whenever friends came to visit. We made forts on top of it and some would charge while others rained down the snowballs. Occasionally the adults would come out and watch me have the time of my life playing on the "snowdrift". They would talk, laugh and I would show off, which usually resulted in being "called down" by my mother. Then we would either go up to the lodge or cabin and the ladies would make hot chocolate for everyone. I would have to remove my gloves, coat, goulashes (overshoes) and shake off all the snow before entering, but that was a small price to pay for the reward! Such small treasures taken for granted then are now invaluable to the both of us.

On January 3, 2011, I received the most wondrous call from Alys Moubry, the granddaughter of Uncle Pug and Aunt Mabel. She was delighted to know that I too shared the experience of growing up in such a loving environment. She shared some pertinent information that assisted in the quest for resolution. Aunt Mabel was born on March 9, 1900. She died on March 27, 1985, due to cancer. Alys stated that her grandmother and my beloved aunt's body was cremated. Her ashes were sprinkled somewhere in a cemetery located in the Punta Gorda, Florida, area. Smitty died in the Sarasota, Florida, region and is buried there.

His birth day was August 21, 1918, and his date of death was April 16, 2001. His last known address was 33982 Punta Gorda, Charlotte County, Florida. His social security number was 369-18-4780.

On January 17, 2011, I received yet another communiqué from Alys Moubry in which she supplied me with more pertinent information on our quest. Her mother, Alys Yvonne (Smith) Geiger, was born on November 17, 1920. She died on November 23, 1986. Alys's father, Robert Hart Geiger, died on January 27, 1971, due to being exposed to Agent Orange while serving his country in Vietnam. He was born on March 6, 1920. He was a highly decorated Lieutenant Colonel.

After my phone call with Alys, it suddenly donned on me that, to the best of my knowledge, we (Alys and I) are the last of that particular Smith generation. A panic came over me and a sense of urgency in regards to my endeavors at capturing the unique experiences of a preteen growing up in the fifties when innocence played upon the land. With renewed vigor I found myself determined to find out more about those times and add them as they are presented to me by others who lived during that timeframe.

This modern world has no clue as to the ecstasy of simplicity and creativity while playing alone or with others.  It is my fervent prayer that through this book, people of my generation and beyond will get a feel of what it was like to grow up in a loving environment which was nestled beneath the whispering pines.

On February 3, 2011, I received an email from Margaret Hodge (daughter of Marie Smith) giving me the email address of Henry (Hank) Cordell.  He attended Red Oak School along with his brothers.  I contacted him in hopes of getting a reunion.  Margaret stated we could have it at her house.

During the week of February 1-4, 2011, the following information was disclosed through research.  Morris Avery 'Smitty' Smith Jr. was laid to rest at Southeastern Crematory.  At this juncture it is unknown whether or not he was buried at Southeastern Funeral Home in Port Richey, Florida, or whether his remains are in the custody of family or is at another cemetery.  He passed away in Charlotte County, Punta Gorda, Florida.  His confirmed date of death is April 6, 2001.  I offer my gratitude to Tammy and Patty at the Vital Statistics Office in Florida, as well as to Jean at Charlotte Cemetery for their efforts in assisting my search. On February 8, 2011, I ordered the death certificate for Aunt Mabel and Smitty in an effort to find their burial locations.

William "Bill" J. DeBeaubien and Donna Louise DeBeaubien last known residence was 720 Long Beach Ct., Punta Gorda, Florida, 33950-7701. Their phone number was listed as (813) 575-0065. Bill and Donna did not have a death certificate on file at the Charlotte County Clerk's office; however, both had probate documents on file. Their place of burial is undetermined at this time until a death certificate is obtained. Some of the neighbors of Bill and Donna DeBeaubien were John and Elsie Andersen, M D Burne, and Harold Deboy. Bill and Donna were married in Baker, Florida, in 1990. The couple was married roughly five years at the time of their deaths. Both Bill and Donna passed away in 1995, roughly 8 months apart.

According to Alys, Morris A. Smith's middle name was Avery. Smitty was Morris Avery Smith Junior. She was unsure as to why his name was listed as Morris J. Smith on a Census Record, unless the "J" stood for Junior. I too recall his name being Morris Avery Smith Junior. Donna had been married to a Jimmy Harper. Upon his death, she remarried her best friend. His name was Bill J. Debeaubien. He was born on April 1, 1911. He was the man I called "Uncle" Bill because he always gave me a dime and took me fishing. Uncle Bill died on April 4, 1995, of prostate cancer. His social security number was 369-07-8855. Donna was born on December 16, 1922, and passed away on December 24, 1995, due to bladder cancer. Their last known residence was Punta Gorda, Charlotte County, Florida. The zip code is 33982. Note that their address was the same as Smittys, indicating they either lived together or very close to one another.

My mother, Dana Blair Chaltas, died on March 26, 1996, due to lung cancer. She suffered for years prior to her yielding to the disease. She was living in Deer Branch, Jeremiah, Kentucky, at the time of her passing. She is buried in the old Lewis Back Cemetery, where one can view the 'holler' where she was born.

I found it so ironic that upon Alys's visit to the lodge; the post (the one I knew as the Talking Post) in the den area was hugged by her as she cried. I did the exact same thing without being privy to the story. Only after I hugged the Talking Post, cried, and patted the old pine log affectionately did the Stiles reveal Alys's reaction to seeing the inside of the lodge. I believe it was and still is a special post layered with sacred memories. It still stands in the parlor area where Uncle Pug built it so many years ago. The circular seat surrounding it is still adorned with magazines and an occasional cushion. That is where I received lectures and love from Uncle Pug, Smitty, and Aunt Mabel. I can still hear its voice as I travel through life's path. When I touched the pole, tears flowed unabatedly. They were tears of appreciation, remembrance, and reflection. Upon sitting on the aged wooden seat, I felt a rush of feelings and emotions bringing back unspoken memories that had been hidden within the confines of the lodge. For a brief second, I felt as if I was once again that youthful child waiting on mother or Aunt Mabel's voice saying, "Come home, it is supper time".

On February 9, 2011, I was delighted to get the following communiqué from my long lost friend, Henry 'Hank' Cordell. His words were like salve to my searching soul. *"David, David, David, Who would have guessed? Yes, I most certainly do remember you, and your Mother. I say that because I remember staying overnight with you at Pine Haven and remember her poise and culture, the atmosphere in your house was so different than that of mine.*

*"John Eckistien was here this summer (our first meeting in 40+years) and we talked of Red Oak and all the kids, pulled out pictures and there you were in your "bowtie", it was at the Christmas Program in the old Log Community Building. I believe my mother had taken the picture to send to my brother George who was in the hospital in Traverse City, he had polio.*

*"Let me quickly go through the kids at the school at that approximate time. Roy Ramsey lives in Detroit...Tom Kann, realtor in Mio...Dennis Kann retired UPS lives in Mio....Bill Kann, Owns Plumbing and Heating in Flint...Jank Kann, retired law*

*enforcement in Lansing...John Eckistien, retired construction worker in Florida...Dan Johns owns a construction company in California...Larry Kruse lived in Flint and Mio and died a few years ago...George Cordell CMW, Watch and gem stone specialist in Allegan until his death at age 44 from complications of his polo...Jim Cordell a retired auto worker 40+years, lives in Detroit...Gib Cordell factory worker in Ripon, Wisconsin.*

*"And if someone would have told me I would have 7+ years of college and 3 degrees and retire after 33+years in education, I would have said 'you're crazy!' The bulk of my years were as Guidance Counselor, I tell you this because it appears that you are connected to education. Aside from a couple of patents, I believe my life ran right from Red Oak School, to retirement, ah, I digress. I married a childhood sweetheart, have 3 children, 5 grandchildren and Deb and I live in Frankfort, Mich.*

*"By Miss Margaret, I think you mean Marie Smith's daughter, she lives just north of us in Empire. I kept in touch with Marie Smith over the years, what a Grand Lady; I say that with all the admiration I possibly can. As for a reunion that WOULD be nice.*

*"Congratulations, I will look for your book and I will certainly follow up on the listed websites below, it was without question a very pleasant surprise to hear from*

*you David, take care and fill in the missing years. Your Ole' Friend, Henry (Hank) Cordell"*

As I read Hank's words from a bygone era, a flood of memories, along with tears, streamed through my mind as well as down this fielder's face. My dear students asked me what was wrong and I shared the good news. They wondered why I was crying and I reminded them of my search. Here was a very large piece of the puzzle filled in by Hank.

On February 14, 2011, I received another notice from my childhood friend. He too recalled a few of our experiences. I offer his words to give you a brief glimpse into the life of children. *"Pure enjoyment (regarding a couple of stories I shared from our book), I can't wait! In 1953, the Board of Education was about to close the Red Oak School, citing too few students (8). A life-long resident of Red Oak (who went to the school himself), named Mr Durey Bailey, wanted the school to stay open, offered our (Cordell) family a rent free house if my parents would move from Pontiac, Michigan to Red Oak, as we had six kids and that would force the board to keep the school open,. It worked, as the school stayed open for almost ten years. It was open when Mr Bailey died several years later.*

*"I too remember a trip to Kenny Roberts " The Jumping Cowboy" on channel 5 in Bay City "...got a nickel in my pocket just to buy some chewin' gum, oh*

322

*sing a song the folks all know, and always keep in style, if you're in love with a pretty little girl, you'll win her by a mile, oh I'm...." Taught this to every one of my Grandkids.*

*I also remember a field trip to see the Mackinac Bridge being build and a Ferry ride across the "Straits", we had to read 100 books, not only did we get to go, we all get a book of our own, mine was the "MIGHTY MAC....a complete history of the building of the Mackinac Bridge. I remember Mrs. Smith taking us to play baseball against another one room school in Comins, it was as if we were playing in the "Series" I remember pitching and John Eckstien catching, we lost miserably, but what an experience. Thank you David, for bringing up all the great "feelings" Your Fiend Hank"*

On February 17, 2011, I received a wonderful surprise from Dorothy Belanger. She is the granddaughter of my former teacher. She sent me a picture of Mrs. Smith just prior to her passing and shared the story of teaching a ninety-two year old to read. The following excerpt testifies to the character of this lady who touched so many lives.

*"She was a wonderful woman and a really special grandmother. She also never lost her love of teaching. While living in her apartment complex she met a 92 year-old neighbor who had never learned to read. Grandma felt you were never too old to learn, and so she began teaching him by borrowing beginning reader*

323

*books which she had given my children, and others she had kept through the years. Before she passed he had gotten a working knowledge of both reading and writing."*

On February 19, 2011, I received the Florida death certificates of Aunt Mabel and Smitty. I immediately wrote Alys what I had discovered. The following is the letter with the pertinent information of their location.

*"Good Afternoon Dear Alys,*

*"I pray all is well with you and yours. I have been bombarded with events, teaching, and court PLUS working around the cabin and old farm...I wish to share the latest with you regarding your family received this day from the Office of Vital Statistics.*

*"I have located the cemeteries and have the certificate of death on your grandmother and Morris Avery 'Smitty' Smith JR. Mabel Alice "Smith passed on March 27, 1985, at the age of eighty-five. The hour of death was 4:30 P.M. She passed from this world to a land of milk and honey at Punta Gorda Medical Center. Her street address was 205 Village Punta Gorda, Florida, 33950. Donna Harper (her youngest daughter) was the informant on the affidavit. Mabel Alice Smith was cremated and her ashes were taken to Lee Memorial Park Crematory, Lehigh Acres, Florida. Her social*

security number was 377-22-4093 and her occupation was listed as a housewife.  She owned her home.

"Morris Avery Smith JR. passed on April 6, 2001.  He was eighty-two years of age.  His birthplace was Gladwin, Michigan.  The records show that he did not serve in the armed forces.  It is my belief that his vision was too poor to pass the eye exam.  His social security number was 369-18-4780.  He died in the same hospital where his mother passed.  The hour of his death was 6:34 P.M.  Barbara M. Beecher Smith (wife) was the informant.  The address was 4300 riverside Drive #205, inside the city limits of Punta Gorda, Florida.  He was in the retail business and was the manager.  He was cremated and the place of disposition is Southeastern Crematory in Punta Gorda, Florida.

"The notification brought relieve but also sadness in the knowledge they will never know what they meant to me.  They were the only true family I ever knew.  I would like for us to purchase a memorial plaque and place it next to Uncle Pug's grave.  When I call (not had much luck lately) maybe we can discuss this and visit Uncle Pug's gravesite together.  I shall put the information in the book and soon sent a RUFF draft to you for your review, input and last minute changes...Our duty as the last generation is to preserve the memory of those we cherish."

On March 2, 2011, I received a delightful correspondence from Alys Moubry. In the letter she noted something about Aunt Mabel which I thought needed to be included in this document. She affirmed that, *"I was at my grandmother's bedside shortly before she died. I had to leave to fly back to Colorado and she died while I was flying home. I remember mom calling me after I got home and telling me grandma had passed."* For some reason, this gave me great comfort knowing that her granddaughter was with her.

I was very pleased and relieved to discover that Smitty had been married. It is my fervent prayer to our Gracious God that he had found happiness. That would give me such a sense of peace to learn he had rediscovered joy and love. I now wonder did he have any children and if so are they aware of how dear their family was to me. My quest shall continue, as I attempt to discover yet another aspect of the Smith's history. One of the items on my bucket list is to go to the cemeteries where Aunt Mabel, and Smitty's ashes are interred and pay my respects. I want them all to know that I am a living legacy to those days where the iron was forged beneath the shadows of the swaying pines. Another is to purchase a memorial stone for Aunt Mabel and place it beside her husband's grave in Flint, Michigan. I feel that is the least I can do to pay tribute to people who invested so much of their time into the development of this unworthy person.

# REFLECTIONS OF CAMELOT

As I reflect back on those days of Camelot, I am sure my mind's eye has glorified the memories of childhood wonders, but in reality is that not what should happen? Is that not the way of childhood reflections? In the overall picture of life we must learn from our disappointments, forgive, forget the days of sorrow, and focus on the simplistic joy of the upbringing. All experiences can make you a better person if you will view them as a blessing. When it is time for you to know, the truth will be revealed. I feel the truth is that without the experiences of yesterday, I would not have been molded into the person I am today. Each building block of my life holds up the structure. It is the foundation which enables us all to continue that building and reinforce those times of joy and sadness.

It never donned upon my being until I was writing this book that I was a product of the fifties. My values, my moral convictions, my attitude, my ethics all stem from that little rural area in Northern Michigan, where even today life is not taken for granted and everyday is an adventure. Very few places on earth offer you the values of yesterday nestled in such scenic splendor as in the Red Oak, Lewiston, Mio areas. Lessons of life FOR life can be learned there and then be passed on to the rising generation.

The greatest lessons you can learn in life is in reality about you. It is not in the classroom but outside of it that we discover and rediscover who we are. My classroom was everywhere, yet nowhere. My lessons that sustained me through all these years were forged at Red Oak, Michigan, where the pine trees waltz with the wind. I was truly blessed to have those six years in which I was able to embrace those who loved me and I loved. The experiences made me a better person and prepared me for a life of helping others.

I thank God every hour for those days and the legacy given unto me by the memories cemented in my mind's eye. I embrace the good, the bad, and the ugly, with the realization that life offers each of us a choice and it falls upon our shoulders the direction in which we choose. I would have been a bird without a song or a butterfly without wings had it not been for the roots I received, and that makes all the difference in my life. The things from our past help mold us and can either help us build a better tomorrow for the rising generation or paralyze us to the point of being stagnant and unfulfilled. The joy of yesteryear maintains me and helps me build the bridges of tomorrow.

On this day, I can honestly say how very thankful I am to all who made my dream of rediscovery come true. To all my fellow classmates who attended Red Oak Elementary, allow me to express my love for each and every one of you. This book is dedicated to you and your descendents, for you are the best part of me and I have never forgotten our times together while in Camelot. To the people of Northern Michigan, I implore you to realize the gifts you possess and share them with others who have lost their way.

I pray that I will continue to hear the voices of yesterday sharing with me my walk upon the wind and maybe when my meandering upon the earth is through, I will leave a legacy for others to follow. As for now, all I know is that due to the voice of longing and my waltz with the wind I am a better person for having revisited the days of shaded memories when I lived in the shadows of the whispering pines. God has truly blessed me in that the person I was, He made new.

# ACKNOWLEDGEMENTS

I have so many people to thank for assisting me on my quest. Mr. and Mrs. Doug and Suzan Anthony-Stiles opened up their lodge to me and allowed to once again step in the footprints of my youth. Mrs. Noreen Stevens from Evart, Michigan, spent hours helping me find the graves of Uncle Pug's mother. She was invaluable in gathering information about the Smith family. The Rustic Inn located on Red Oak Road (M489) offered their help and Joann, a lovely young waitress, made calls to local people to find my former classmates. Mrs. Carol also talked to others on my behalf. To the unknown lady in an antique shop in Lewiston, Michigan, I thank you so much. To the funeral directors that I bombarded with questions, the Historical Societies I emailed, and to the school district I solicited, as I looked for Marie Smith and others, I am in your debt. Special thanks go to Mio County Court Clerk, Becky & Thelma of Flint Memorial Park. I must acknowledge Miss Bambi Sowards, who encouraged me, researched with me and for me, and who believed in my vision quest even when I began to doubt my abilities. I owe her my eternal gratitude and a debt that I shall continue to pay for as long as I live. Special thanks go to Margaret Hodge, Hank Cordell, Alys Moubry, and Dorothy Belanger.

# AUTHOR'S COMMENTS

Somewhere out there is a document, a person or agency who will know something. Every little lead is not too small. It will take time and determination but you will rediscover your roots. In regard to research, there are several things I have learned along the way. I offer them to you in hopes they will help expedite your search. Remember this:

- Several documents spelled my aunt's name Mabel or Mable. I chose Mabel because it was on most of the documents, such as the deed and Uncle Pug's death certificate.
- Seek help from professionals, historical societies of the area, local realtors, business owners, and city officials.
- Research the newspaper archives of the area and find the location of pertinent records, such as birth, death, divorce, and public data.
- Surround yourself with helpful people and genuinely offer your gratitude to them. So many people were helpful and gave of their time to assist me in my quest. I offer a special thanks of gratitude to the fine people of Oakland Court House, Pontiac Clerk's Office, Mio Court Clerk's Office, Rustic Inn, Evart Library and Museum who did a wonderful job in assisting in my the search.

- After driving over five hundred miles one way to research, I was disappointed with the visit to Flint County Clerk's Office by the lack of sensitivity and assistance. You will encounter those who do not enjoy their profession or lack professional courtesy skills. In spite of such obstacles, continue your search.

- Keep a positive attitude and don't give up when you encounter your first obstacle. You will hit walls. Stop, think, and refocus. Keep searching for the answers are out there.

- Special thanks to Thelma Miller from Flint Memorial Cemetery who went out of her way to help me locate the grave of Morris A. Smith (Uncle Pug), and Norris C. Smith.

- Places to search include deeds, survey maps, death records, birth certificates (these can be hard to obtain), wills, websites such as ancestry.com, and interviews of community members.

- I found posting flyers with relevant information being requested on them helpful as well. Posting a circular at local stores, restaurants, senior citizens, etc. proved to be a valued asset.

- Remember if one angle of research doesn't pan out for you, try another method. Look at family names and secure books about surnames and lineages.

- I found that letter writing, once you find a point of contact, gets the person of the area involved in your research. I offer my thanks to Ms. Karen Sue Smith for her contributions in my search for Marie Smith. My special thanks to Mrs. Marie Smith's daughter, Margaret Smith Hodge, for her contributions. Her information was most helpful.

- Contact funeral homes, cemeteries, floral shops that place wreaths and flowers on graves. They have a wealth of information.

- Utilize secure social networking such as Facebook, Ancestry.com, Twitter, and other relevant sites. Post ad in local papers where you think your ancestor might have lived or is buried.

- Most cities have a Chamber of Commerce. They are an excellent source to explore. They have always been friendly and supportive in my research.

- Ask about family Bibles. They usually have a wealth of information within their covers.

- Another avenue you can pursue is to obtain information from the school district regarding class reunions. Sometimes pertinent information about the school's history, those who attended the school and even addresses can be discovered.

- My thanks go to Gloria from Gulf Pines Memorial Park, who took it upon herself to research her area in an effort to find the records on Mabel and her son, Morris A. Smith Junior. Such unselfish altruistic acts will be rewarded by being passed forward.

- My undying gratitude to Mrs. Alys Moubry, the only grandchild of my beloved Uncle Pug and Aunt Mable, for her assistance and encouragement regarding the preservation efforts of this historical timeframe and of paying homage to her grandparents. Not only did she afford me information but I know have a direct link to our common past and a new cousin.

- To my dear long lost friend, Hank Cordell, thank you for filling in so many spaces in my life. Remember those people who shared common experiences. They possess a wealth of information.

- To my Red Oak Classmates, I offer my undying devotion and pray that we will someday play upon the fields of glory together. Your legacy continues.

- To Dorothy Belanger I thank you for sharing your grandmother and my teacher with me. Your stories and picture filled a void that I shall not forget.

- Research old cemetery records and seek assistance from the care takers. They are a wealth of information and will gladly guide you along during your quest.

- Pray for guidance is always important and never think a lead is too small, no matter how insignificant it might seem to you. Follow your heart, therein lies your destiny.
- Finally, never give up the quest, no matter how long it takes. Each tidbit builds the story, the genealogy, and helps preserve history/heritage for the rising generation.

# Childhood Images

(Author in his youth)

(Author earning his nickname, Butch)

(Mother by her apartment in Detroit)

(7/11/2010-Author's visit to childhood home)

*NOTE*: Finally I wish to express my deepest heartfelt thanks to Suzan and Doug Stiles. They allowed me an opportunity for rediscovery and, more importantly, closure to a chapter of my life that was my foundation and finest hour.

"Pine Ridge Lodge remains open three hundred sixty-five (365) days a year; we just manage it as it happens. Much as during its origination, hunting and fly fishing are very popular activities of our guests. We also host many family retreats, corporate meetings, romantic weekend getaways, reunions, mushroom hunts, nature lovers, cross country skiers, motorcyclists, bird watchers, tourists, snowmobilers, golfers, and bikers. Several come to visit and just sit by the fire, read, or play a game of Scrabble." For a wondrous time of family fun or an unforgettable getaway, remember to visit the place where I lived while in the shadows of the whispering pines.

http://www.pineridgelodgemi.com/

(The Stiles at home)

# PHOTOS OF LODGE LIFE

The following pictures are courtesy of Alys Moubry, the only grandchild of the Smiths. They represent a window into the past and the details offer clues of a gentler time in America.

(Lodge Facing North)

(Lodge Porch)

(Pictures of the lodge)

(Frosty-upper left; middle right)

(Note: Upper left-hand picture: old trailer that
was beside the cabin)

(The Smith Family-Smitty on Right)

(Mabel Smith)

(Uncle Pug and Aunt Mable)

Венгрия Будапешт 1984

# ONLY THE BEGINNING

Some people have asked me what I have discovered about myself during this quest. That is a loaded question. There have been so many things but the greatest is closure. You see, I was uprooted from a place I dearly loved and was never given an explanation as to what happened or why did we move. Those dear friends who remained at Red Oak School went on to high school together and have taken for granted the bond that, for me, was broken. There was a void filled with questions that I desperately needed to have answered. Some of the questions have been answered, while others linger. So in essence the completion of this book is, in reality, only the beginning for me.

I conclude with the prayer that you, dear reader, will recognize how important the moments in your life are and record them for your family, friends, and others to realize the uniqueness and potential within each of us. We must allow each day to mold us to be a better person and once we have obtained our higher calling, it is then that we must give it away to others so that they can find their uniqueness. In this manner we contribute a link to the future by sharing our past. Be blessed as is God's intent.

In the Shadows of the Pines

The childlike seedling saw his father fall.
His eyes would shine no more.
A void filled the valley and the glen looked barren
But salvation came upon the wind.

The sapling struggled with the wonders of growth
As he was nurtured from above.
The shadows hid his youthful existence
Within the shelter of the glen, he smiled.

Oh youthful slender with the joys of innocence
Running as pristine as the AuSable on its trek to
the Huron.
Surrounded by potential, the sapling grew,
Protected from the storms blown by wayward
winds.

Suddenly uprooted from the six years of Camelot's
glory,
The sapling fell among barren dust.
He struggled to survive and hid from the evil
Only to become entangled with webs of sorrow.

In autumn's light the now grown oak remembered
The land which had cultivated his character.
When he tumbled, his spirit was uprooted and
returned
To rest in the shadows of the whispering pines.

The proceeding poem came to me on the whisper of the wind and I thought it fitting to end this portion of my saga. We are nothing more than memories and vapors. We must cherish life and I beg you to embrace each moment as if it was your last. For you will never know when you might be uprooted and find yourself running from the storm.

(The Glen of my youth)

**June 56 at 8ᵗʰ Grade Graduation**

(Left to right-Jim Cordell, John Eckstein, Gib Cordell, George Cordell, Carl Aygffe, Jack Kann, Roy Ramsey, Bill Kann, ?, Hank Cordell, David Chaltas, Tom Kann)

**Christmas 58**
(Left to right-Bill Kann, Jack Kann, Dan Johns,
Larry Krause, David Chaltas, Gib Cordell, John
Eckstein, Jim Cordell, Hank Cordell, Dennis
Kann)

I wish to offer a special appreciation to Hank
Cordell, who shared so many memories with me
and shook some of the cobwebs from my
remembrances.

## Mysterious Ways

God works in mysterious ways. On July 20, 2014, I was in northern Michigan, visiting old haunts and looking at property in the area. My cousin, Pete Kyle, called me and stated he had some pictures he found of me when I was a child that belonged to his mother (my Aunt Ellie). Little did I realize the treasures he was about to give me.

I met him in the Lexington Cemetery beside his parents' graves. He came up to me with that usual smile, hugged me and we talked for awhile. Then he walked over and got a folder out of his truck. Inside the folder were not only pictures of me but more importantly, one of my father and mother. I had not seen a picture of my father and after sixty-one years, I now have an image of him and my mother.

This will always be a family heirloom and I am in debt to an unselfish cousin who found the pictures his mother had taken care of for all these years. I felt compelled and led to place them in this book. I offer them to you, dear reader, and pray you may find the pieces of the puzzle in your life.

(Inside Cabin)

(Author, Russell, and Arlin Blair: Detroit, 1959)

Mr. and Mrs. Phillip Chaltas
(Dana-17 years old Phillip 60 years old)

(Author at 2 days old)

(Author-age unknown)

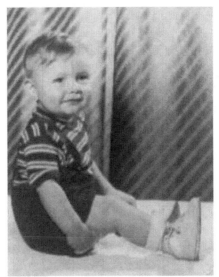

(Author at 1 year of age; Taken at Martin Studios,6505
Second Street, Detroit, Michigan) )

(Author at 22 months-May 7, 1949. Mother had written
on the back of the picture to her sister, Ella: "This is just
like him He had been pulling at his hat and had it all
crooked.)

(Author on Easter Sunday-May 9, 1950)

(Taken in Landlord's Yard: Author at 2 ½)

(Taken in Front of Father's Restaurant in Greek Town,
Downtown Detroit: May 7, 1949)

(Mother and Me)

(Mother, Author, and Lucky in our front yard below
Pine Haven Lodge in September of 1956)

(Author September 56)

(Me & Danny Johns Playing in Front Yard: June 59)

(The Lone Ranger!  September 1956)

365

(Christmas in the Cabin!)

(My Beloved Teacher, Mrs. Marie Smith, with
Unknown Students & Author: June of 59)

(Mother in Sept of 56)

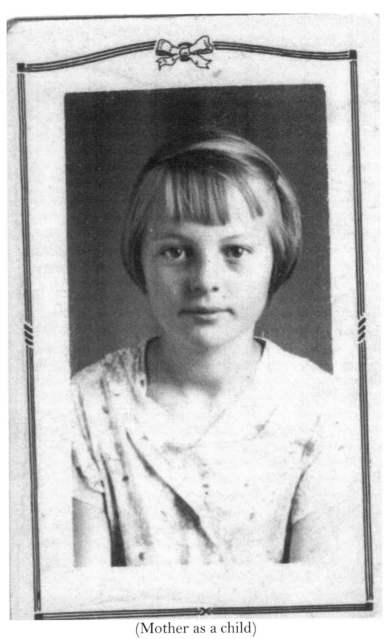

(Mother as a child)

(Opal Back and Mother)

**"Precious memories, how the linger
How they ever fill my soul..."**

{Dedicated to my grandchildren and future generations
that follow...}

Made in the USA
Monee, IL
28 September 2020